GW00675935

SOCIC

The Seductive Practices and Dark Psychology of
Sociopaths

(Narcissist and Sociopath Personality Disorders
Explained)

Felipe Karl

Published by John Kembrey

Felipe Karl

All Rights Reserved

Sociopath: The Seductive Practices and Dark Psychology of Sociopaths (Narcissist and Sociopath Personality Disorders Explained)

ISBN 978-1-77485-127-2

Legal & Disclaimer

The information contained in this book is not designed to replace or take the place of any form of medicine or professional medical advice. The information in this book has been provided for educational and entertainment purposes only.

The information contained in this book has been compiled from sources deemed reliable, and it is accurate to the best of the Author's knowledge; however, the Author cannot guarantee its accuracy and validity and cannot be held liable for any errors or omissions. Changes are periodically made to this book. You must consult your doctor or get professional medical advice before using any of the suggested remedies, techniques, or information in this book.

Upon using the information contained in this book, you agree to hold harmless the Author from and against any damages, costs, and expenses, including any legal fees potentially resulting from the application of any of the information provided by this guide. This disclaimer applies to any damages or injury caused by the use and application, whether directly or indirectly, of any advice or information presented, whether for breach of contract, tort, negligence, personal injury, criminal intent, or under any other cause of action.

You agree to accept all risks of using the information presented inside this book. You need to consult a professional medical practitioner in order to ensure you are both able and healthy enough to participate in this program.

Table of Contents

Chapter 1: Differences In Sociopath, Psychopath, Sociopathy And Aspd

There are a great many different disorders which come under the umbrella of mental health disorders. These main types are:

• Anxiety – Anxious response to certain stimuli is a fairly common issue and classed as a mental health issue.

• Mood – Extreme moods for long periods of time or very fast mood changes.

• Psychotic – This is usually displayed via seeing and believing in things which are not there; including hallucinations and delusions.

• Eating Disorders – Extreme emotional reaction to food.

- Addictions – People can become addicted to anything and this can have an extremely detrimental effect on their life.

- Obsessive Compulsive Disorders – Fear forces people to repeat a set of actions a specific number of times. The fear and the reaction are unique to each person.

- Post traumatic Stress Disorder – This is the result of an extreme situation and can have long lasting effects.

- Personality Disorders – Society sets a standard of acceptable personality traits, based on the average person. People with a personality disorder exist on an extreme level of this range.

The sociopath is someone who has a personality disorder; they operate in the extreme range of the normal emotional response.

Sociopathy is simply the term for the disorder, whilst the term sociopath is used for a specific person with the sociopathy disorder. Many medical professionals have now taken to using the term Antisocial Personality Disorder instead of the word sociopath or sociopathy. This is simple because the disorder is far more complicated that the classic image which is often attached to the word sociopath or psychopath. Not all sociopaths are criminals; many of these people manage to live successful, productive lives. In fact, many people with this personality disorder are highly intelligent; it is this which enables them to understand other people and manipulate them according to their needs. Their intelligence and charisma in their public persona will allow them to become a leader in business, a high ranking political figure or even a celebrity. This is possible due to both their intelligence and their inability to consider other people. There are several key distinctions between a sociopath and a psychopath:

• Organisation. This is a key difference in these two personality types. A sociopath will have o regard for other people's feelings, but they will be haphazard and reactive in their approach to any issue. In fact, many of their actions are spontaneous; one action leads to another and so on. A sociopath will live in the moment, regardless of the effect of that moment on the people around them. In contrast a psychopath will be highly organised, every action they take will be carefully thought out beforehand. They will usually devise contingency plans and will remain cool and calm; whatever the situation.

• Attachments – Despite the inability to comprehend the effect of their actions on others, a sociopath is capable of forming a relationship with one other or even a small group. However, these relationships will revolve around the sociopath and can be exceptionally volatile. As well as being prone to angry outbursts they are usually nervous and often agitated. The result is that many relationships are short term. In contrast the psychopath will be completely unable to form an emotional attachment. However, they will be able to mimic these emotions in order to gain people's trust and achieve their own aims.

• Image – The sociopath's personality will usually result in them appearing disturbed; or at the least odd, in comparison to the average person. This will make others feel wary of spending too much time with them as they are unpredictable. They often move from job to job and even place to place. The psychopath is far more integrated into society. Their ability to act the part will enable them to build a family, hold down a good job and even build a business empire. However, all their actions will be based upon an act, as part of a grand plan.

• Cause – The cause of sociopathy is thought to be a result of nurture; the environment in which someone has grown up in. It is believed that this can have a serious affect on any person and influence the way they view life and other people. Anyone who has been subjected to a massive trauma, particularly in childhood, or even emotional and physical abuse is at risk of developing a sociopath personality. In effect, these situations encourage people to switch off their emotions and learn to distance themselves from both their emotions and other people. A psychopath is generally believed to be a product of nature. Research continues into this delicate field but it is thought that a psychopath has undeveloped areas of their brain, in particular the part which controls impulses and emotions. Whilst this disorder is usually something you are born with, it is also possible to damage your brain in an accident and develop a psychopathic personality.

• Danger Level – A sociopath will not understand the effect of their actions on others and will not feel any emotion if they harm others. However, as this is a condition that has been learnt, rather than been born with, there is still an understanding of the rules and regulations of society. A sociopath will not believe these rules apply to themselves. However, a psychopath will have no regard for the law and are able to remove their actions from their emotions. They can reason that anything is permissible if it is necessary to achieve their goals. Even if the course of action they intend to take is particularly bad. This makes a psychopath very dangerous to those around them; in fact many of the most famous serial killers have been confirmed as psychopaths.

• Education – A sociopath is usually lacking in concentration and is easily bored. This results in a lack of education when growing up. Children who rebel against the rules and regulations are often seen as antisocial, in the more extreme cases this is likely to be due to the personality disorder. In fact, as many as four percent of the population have sociopath personalities. As adults they will often reflect the classic 'thug'. Someone with a psychopathic personality will have integrated with society and seen the importance of an education. They will generally be well educated and able to control their behaviour in order to bide their time and make their move at the right time.

The differences between the two disorders are relatively small; however they are significant in understanding the condition and offering treatment. A sociopath, who is a product of their environment, needs to have a carefully structured plan to assist them in adjusting to a normal life. It is believed that the ability to display empathy is buried and not gone completely; this makes it reasonable to assume that the right treatment; counselling and even medication can help someone with this disorder to become more in touch with their feelings and other people's. A psychopath cannot be treated in the same way as their brains are underdeveloped and the emotive response required is not there.

Both disorders are recognised as being an antisocial personality disorder (ASPD). The media has also highlighted the connection between psychopaths and people who are criminals; it has even been seen in a host of movies, such as 'Hannibal'. However, this book will enable you to recognise a sociopath and, by default, a psychopath; but this does not mean they are a criminal.

There are thousands of people who live with antisocial personality disorder and never commit a crime. It is also worth noting that a psychotic personality is not the same as a psychopath. The psychopath can integrate fully into society and appear to have emotions; the psychotic person cannot; they are completely disconnected from society; these are the types of people who will hear voices; which may instruct them to commit crimes.

Both psychopathy and sociopathy are classified as antisocial personality disorders as people with these disorders are unable to react in what is perceived to a normal response. Unfortunately a sociopath is not aware that they are acting outside of the perceived norm; even if you tell them. This means they are unlikely to seek out treatment for a condition they did not know they had. A psychopath may be aware that they have the disorder but are unlikely to seek treatment unless they see it as beneficial for some reason. Even if they do seek treatment there is no guarantee that they will provide truthful information to the medical professional.

Chapter 2: What Is Psychopathy And How Not To Confuse It With Sociopathy

One of the most common misconceptions when people hear about sociopath, is that it's just similar to psychopath. Sometimes when we hear people being diagnosed with sociopathy we directly relate it for them having psychopathy or the other way around. And what's worse is that some people tend to generalize their conditions. That they are all similar, hungry for violence, killing machines and insane. When you are around people who undergo either of the two conditions, it is very important that you know the basics of their condition, not only for you to become more knowledgeable but also for your own safety.

It may be because they have some similarities when it comes to some behavioral actions, but in reality it is like calling dogs and cats similar just because they both have fur and paws. When it comes to this matters you should be careful to what you say and make sure that you have enough knowledge about it. For you to know more about the differences between psychopathy and sociopathy, here are some of the information that will help you differentiate one from the other.

Definition

To start, let us first define what psychopathy and sociopathy is. When we say psychopathy it refers to a personality disorder that causes people to be anti-social. The major contribution for psychopathy is genetics. Such cases are hereditary especially of those who have parents or relatives having the same condition. There are many tests who can examine of a kid has a tendency to have psychopathy if his or her parents have history. It may surprise you that they even get to have kids but that is true. With proper medication, series of therapies and continuous guidance, those who have psychopathy may still be able to live a normal life and have their own family. In Cases such as this, it is very important that as early as possible, the child will be monitored for any symptoms or possibility of attaining the same disorder.

When psychologists refer to this condition, what they mostly look at are the person's innate condition and not on what kind of environment he or she is exposed to. We may have seen many movies referring to psychopaths as those who have high disposition to violence but aside from this, there are still many things that we do not know about this condition. Thanks to the many existing medical breakthroughs and innovative programs dedicated to help those who have the same condition little by little experts are gaining more knowledge about what psychopathy is and the possible cure or if not steps on how to mitigate its effect.

On the other hand, when we say sociopathy, it is still a personality disorder leading for those under this condition to be anti-social. But psychologists refer the term sociopath to those who became anti-social because of their experiences in life. Such condition is mainly influenced by what they believe in their life, can be caused by a brain injury or to their external environment. Other external environment factors are being neglected in the family, being exposed to peers who are also anti-social, low self-confidence, high intelligence even poverty can also be a factor. If you think about it, what is good about sociopathy is that it can still be changed. People under this condition can still be diagnosed under continuous therapy and the factors affecting sociopathy can still be controlled. Similar to psychopathy factors resulting to this condition are yet to be known and with continuous efforts soon more information will be available for people to fully understand these conditions, their causes, symptoms and most of all cure.

Difference

Both of these anti-social personality may result to violence if not well taken care of. But there are therapies well designed for these conditions, where both are cases are treated differently. Even those who are in authority treat their cases differently from one another. For there are some instances that are present in the cases of psychopathy that is not present in sociopathy and so is true in vice versa. As a matter of fact, you might even be amazed as to how different they are from one another that after this, you will not be having difficulties differentiating psychopathy from sociopathy.

People who undergo psychopathy suffers from anti-social personality, they tend to be delusional and have even lost their ability to feel empathy or recognize their own conscience. While those of sociopathy are generally anti-social only. When it comes to the source of the illness psychopathy is derived from genetics, an innate condition of the person. While sociopathy are caused by the negative social environment the person has long been exposed to. Psychopathy is embedded within the person and sociopathy being mainly influenced by their own environment both internal and external. What most people know about both conditions is that they tend to be violent most of the time. Although it can be said that it is true, it is psychopathy that has higher inclination towards violence and sociopathy is more varied.

Both conditions also make the person be impulsive most of time. Although when it comes to the level of being impulsive sociopathy is higher while psychopathy's impulsiveness may be varied or to the point become generally low. Even their behavior differs, as sociopaths have erratic behavior as to compared to sociopaths who can actually control their own behavior. As you can see, people who have sociopathy are mostly unrelaxed and impulsive when making decisions and most especially on the way they act. In terms of criminal records, the sociopaths sometimes leaves clues in the crime scene due to their impulsiveness and uncertain actions. While the psychopaths are more controlled and even has the tendency to make participation to criminal actions with well planned schemes to the point that even the risks were minimized to avoid leaving of evidences or being exposed to the crime.

In terms of career it is the psychopaths that are successful in finding jobs and negotiating. They like maintaining connections if and only if they are benefited the most. They are able to know how people feel and how they are being controlled by emotions. And because they do not have the ability to feel the same emotions yet know what they do to a person, psychopaths tend to use this to play with people and use them to do their bidding. Cases of abuse, physical violence and emotional violence are often the results of this scheme. While sociopaths are not as well organized as the psychopaths making them unable to keep a steady job, be with the same people or even stay home for a long time.

Their criminal predispositions also differ as they both have different takes on their criminal behavior. Because of their impulsive behavior, sociopaths take violence whenever they feel like doing so or if there are even a slightest chance to do so, they will take it. They do not think twice before they take action, making them extremely risk takers. On the part of the psychopaths however, having been able to control their behavior, they first plan their motives before taking an action. They will make sure that risks are well minimized and that as much as possible cover ups are well made. They will not make any action when they are still unsure of the possible outcome, they first plan before executing the crime making them less susceptible being guilty in the crime.

As both of them are having difficulties socializing with people, there will still be times that they try but more often than not, for the opportunity to inflict violence. For sociopaths, they can pretend to be having normal conversations with people.

To the point that they can even be sympathetic to people who are their target of violence. A scheme well played by them. However, when they hurt a family, friend or those dear to them, they may still be able to feel guilty. In the case of psychopaths, they are not able to socialize to people when it would not benefit them. They only make connections for their own good. Since they do not feel empathy they may hurt their family, friends or those dear to them without even feeling guilty or sympathetic.

Similarities

Even with their behavioral disorder, both sociopathy and psychopathy may still be cured or if not alleviated at some point. As you know there are specialized therapies designed for each cases and both treatments, although different in terms of method, requires continues guidance. There are also medicated pills for their progress in treatment that are similar for both cases. All of these medications can only be accessed with proper and strict diagnosis and can only be taken with the guidance of those parties concerned. It may be a family member, a psychologist or those who are in authority.

In terms of being manipulative both of them are also good at these schemes. They may not be able to stand socializing for a long time but when completely motivated for their need for violence or any personal intentions. They are very observant and keen at keeping tabs on their target of interest. Not to mention that both psychopaths and sociopaths are also charming that they are able to bend people easily. Even if those people doesn't want to, they have no choice but to fall for the charisma of those who are under these conditions. And even if they're anti-social, they may still be able to keep connections to a few people given that it is for their own interest or benefit.

Researches have also shown that in both cases of psychopathy and sociopathy the symptoms starts to resurface when the people diagnosed under these conditions reaches fifteen years of age. There have also been patterns observed on both parties that shows early warnings that the person may be suffering under behavioral disorder, either psychopathy or sociopathy.

The early stage can be observed when they show cruelty to animals to the point of killing them not for fun but for no apparent reason at all. You may have seen lots of videos in the internet about human cruelty to animals and most of them, after series of examinations have been diagnosed with psychopathy or sociopathy. Next is them not being able to be sympathetic to people around them and lastly not care about anyone else but for themselves. As if they live only for themselves and other people are irrelevant even their lives. All of these symptoms are experienced by persons who have either psychopathy or sociopathy.

Finally, even a person has sociopathy or psychology, he or she may still be able to build his or her own family. Nowadays, due to information dissemination, medications and well organized therapies, those who are suffering from these conditions may still be able to live a normal life and build their own family. With continuous medication, therapy sessions and guidance they may still be able to maintain living a normal life. Both conditions have cure readily available, if only the relatives of those who are suffering from these conditions do an effort to save them before the effect of psychopathy or sociopathy becomes irreversible. Also, those who suffer from both conditions are not insane or mentally disabled. They are both anti-social, not crazy and having psychotic breakdowns. One thing that all of us should be remembering.

Now that you know about the basic information about the difference of psychopathy and sociopathy it will now be easier for you to understand their behavior and the reason behind their actions. One of the common mistakes people do is to generalize that the character of sociopaths are just similar to sociopaths. Some may not even know what psychopaths are or what sociopaths are. The more you know about their difference the easier it will be for you to recognize which is which and you can then guard yourselves around them.

Chapter 3: Defying Deception

One of the worst characteristics of a sociopath is their need to deceive others through lies. Sociopaths can lie to others in many different ways. A sociopath can be described as a compulsive liar. These lies are told compulsively and the sociopath often has no control of the lies that are being told to others. Sociopaths will lie to your face even when they don't have to and it won't phase them at all. Most individuals feel regret and remorse after telling a lie. Now, this doesn't apply to all individuals. Some individuals are able to tell lies and deceive others, not feel any remorse and not be a sociopath. It's important to understand that there are multiple characteristics that come into play when identifying a sociopath. The difference between liars and sociopaths is that liars lie usually to get out of something. For example, a man may lie to a woman when asked whether or not he has committed adultery because he's afraid of the repercussions. A liar lies to protect himself, he lies to keep himself out of trouble or he lies to prevent others from being hurt. In contrast to a general liar, a sociopath lies just for the sake of lying. When people lie and they're not a sociopath, they often lie simply because they are afraid to face the truth and be honest with others about certain issues. For example, when a child begins to lie at a young age in order to not get in trouble, they may continue to lie throughout their lives, lies become a way of surviving life. To be clear, these lies are usually told in order to protect themselves, the lies are not intentionally told to hurt others. Individuals may lie to look better to others, they may exaggerate a situation in order to make it seem more exciting. There are many reasons why liars lie, but one reason is not usually to hurt others and cause others pain. The lies are usually told to improve a situation and either make things better or cover something up.

A sociopath simply lies to see if he can trick people and make them believe what he is saying. The lies become a twisted game from the sociopath and the fact that he does not have empathy for others makes this game even more intriguing and satisfying for the sociopath. This deceiving game is incredibly addicting for sociopaths. They are drawn to the lies and they feed off of deceiving others. The fact that these lies affect others and often cause a great deal of pain does not affect the sociopath at all. These individuals feel absolutely no remorse for the lies and they become intrigued by tricking as many people as possible. These tricks are often so painful for others because they ultimately believe the sociopath and what he's saying only to find out that everything said was a lie. Sociopaths are able to completely fabricate stories out of small events that may occur day to day. Some lies may be so in depth that many individuals believe these lies and in fact the sociopath believes his own lies as well. That being said, some lies will be less severe than others. That being said, it doesn't take away from the lies that are being told day to day, what these means is that there are more severe lies that physically hurt others or ruin their lives that sociopaths tell in order to cause harm upon others.

While some lies may not be serious, they may in fact be minor lies, white lies even, other lies are very severe and may include lies about severe, painful acts done to others. Sociopaths obviously have other very disturbing traits and characteristics but they all intertwine with the other. For example, a sociopath might commit a crime such as murder, theft, rape or something just as severe and when they are asked if they committed the crime they will lie or fabricate lies that never occurred. The disturbing aspect of this is that if a sociopath does commit a crime and won't admit to the wrong doing, it becomes difficult to pinpoint evidence that he in fact is guilty. In fact, sociopaths can often be so manipulative that they are able to actually convince others that they had no part in committing the act. The worst part about sociopaths and their repetitive lies is that they are so convincing that others actually believe them and what they're saying. These pathological liars are incredibly charming and convincing. It makes it hard for those who are not familiar with them, not to believe everything they're saying. The whole point of lying for a sociopath is to gain something from these lies. The sociopath actually feels as though he has gained something from the lies if he knows that he has caused pain upon someone. This pain provides satisfaction for the sociopath. Although these pathological liars understand that their lies hurt others, they understand how much pain they can cause and the simply do not care or feel any empathy for those in pain. They know what's right and wrong and continue to choose the lies because this ultimately satisfies them. This sick and twisted behavior is often recognized when it's too late and the pathological liar has already done enough damage to create a great deal of pain upon others. Sociopaths feel nothing regarding their actions. They do not feel any remorse, they do not feel any pain or guilt, they only feel satisfaction when they are able to get others to do things for them such as lie, cheat and steal.

These lies told by sociopaths can be just about anything. Keep in mind that a sociopath isn't necessarily a murder, he may very well be, but he doesn't have to be. A sociopath can definitely be someone less severe than a murderer. For example, a sociopath may be your boyfriend, your boss or even your best friend, it just may take you a while to realize these behaviors and character traits. Maybe your boyfriend led you to believe that he graduated from Yale with a degree in English but you've never actually seen a diploma, transcript, or anything else related to that school. Your boyfriend may have even told you that he was a pro dirt bike rider when he was younger and that he's never been married. Eventually you may find out that he lied about all of these things. Maybe your best friend completely fabricated her childhood, education and other aspects of her life, well while these individuals may in fact be compulsive liars, these are definitely red flags and should be investigated in depth to make sure they are just compulsive liars and not sociopaths. Once you're aware of what and who you're dealing with, there are signs that you will be able to look for and you may even be able to catch the sociopath in a lie or two. Sociopaths often tell people different stories. The story may change from person to person and if you pay close attention to what the sociopath is telling to others as well as yourself, you may be able to confront the sociopath with this information. That being said, the sociopath most likely will not admit to the lie, they will just create other lies to mislead you and make you forget that you actually caught them in a lie. Confronting a sociopath with their lies is difficult because the lying will continue.

Chapter 4: The Affect Of Living With A Personality Disorder

Someone who has a personality disorder may not be aware of their disorder, but that will not stop it from having an impact on their life and the lives of those around them. One person's disorder can seriously affect the ability for many people, particularly their family, to live a normal life. The following issues are all common for someone who is dealing with a personality and their family:

Relationship Issues

Anyone who has a personality disorder is likely to have difficult forming relationships with others. This may be because they are too needy and anxious and others cannot deal with their demands over a long period of time, alternatively, this can be because they have a short attention span and quickly lose interest in their latest best friend and move on to a new one. The result is a lack of deep friendship and anyone to support or help them in difficult times.

Family and long term friends (people who have been around since before the condition became obvious) usually end up dealing with the fall out of these short term relationships and having to make available vast amounts of their own time in order to support the sufferer. This can make it difficult for the family to live normal lives and maintain their own relationships.

For the sanity of all those involved it is essential to have a plan and share the responsibility of looking after and being there for the loved one who is suffering. This is the only way that everyone involved can maintain both their own sanity and relationships of their own.

The larger the family and the more couples which exist the more lives which can be affected by this issue.

Needy

It is common for sufferers with personality disorders to become very needy of the support, both physical and mental which is offered by their loved ones. Many sufferers desperately need to feel important or loved and need to reassured constantly that this remains the case. This constant reassurance can be physically and emotionally draining for everyone involved.

The sufferer will struggle to live their own life, in fact it is highly likely that their need for reassurance or confirmation of their abilities will be demanding enough to that they will need to have support at home, or even share a home with someone who cares.

Being needy will also be a huge hindrance to building a relationship of any sort with new people; someone who is needy will come across as clingy and will jump far ahead of the current relationship and start planning for a distant future event. This action will be to confirm the presence of someone special in their life, but, will in fact, come across as desperate and is likely to have people leaving the relationship before they have given it a proper chance.

Inability to Let Go

People with personality disorders are often paranoid and suspicious of the world around them. They are, however, trusting and committed to those they have known for a long time. Sufferers generally have very few people that they really connect with; this usually means that it is very easy for a sufferer to fixate on those that do care; and are already a part of their life. Even if they have the opportunity to create new relationships they will be very reluctant to let go off the relationships which are already established.

This can make it very difficult for those who are looking after a sufferer and attempting to help them recover. Being constantly need and relied upon will make it very difficult for them to continue with their existing friendships or build relationships of their own. Of course, they cannot simply leave a loved one suffering as, despite the inconvenience, they love them and are trying to help them. In addition they are likely to suffer from guilt and anxiety as to how someone with a personality disorder will cope without their help.

Stress

The demands on your time and the effort which is needed to keep your loved one safe and happy can be physically and emotionally draining. Being constantly aware of their needs and on call to help when needed, can place a huge amount of stress on your body. You will be attempting to juggle your own career, possibly your own family and a variety of other commitments. Dealing with all of this on a daily basis without giving yourself time to relax and recuperate will leave you stressed out and is likely to make you ill. At which point you will be of no help to anyone!

Your loved one who is suffering from a personality disorder will also be feeling the stress of relying on others, but they will have a need for your assistance and derive comfort from your presence and support.

It is essential that you and the person who is suffering do something to alleviate your stress, this can be together or separately as long as it is an opportunity not to think about the issues you are dealing with.

Work Problems

Unfortunately it can be very difficult for people suffering with a personality disorder to make a connection with others and this can seriously affect their ability to secure and retain a job of any sort. If they have been in the job role before their personality disorder became an issue then their employer may offer some support during a difficult period. However, many types of personality disorders lead to anxiety and a mistrust of those around them. If they feel that their colleagues are constantly plotting against them they will become more stressed and more erratic in their behaviour. This is likely to result in the loss of their job and further self-esteem issues.

Alternatively, those with a personality disorder which requires them to be the centre of attention will need to undertake more and more ridiculous activities in order to stay the centre of attention. Eventually these activities will impact on their work and cause issues.

It is important to remember that those who are offering care and support will face their own employment challenges. A needy loved one with a personality disorder can want your help at all sorts of times of the day and your employer may need to be very understanding to tolerate this and allow you flexible working. If not your own job may be at risk.

Emotional Distress & Despair

Some people with personality disorders know they have an issue but do not know how to deal with it; even with the care and support of loved ones and medical professionals. It can be a long road to recovery and it can seem almost impossible much of the time. Thinking about this can lead to emotional distress and even depression for both the sufferer and those who are doing their best to help them.

Sufferers may find it worse as they will also feel the anxiety of their condition and the stress and burden they are placing on others; of course, many sufferers do not see this part of the problem.

The emotional burden on a loved one can be strenuous and you will need your own support if you are to deal with it and not make yourself ill in the process.

It can be very difficult to monitor the amount of emotional distress you are under; to many people it will not be obvious until you are also struggling. This is why it is essential for anyone supporting someone with a personality disorder to remember that the most important person to look after is yourself; you cannot help anyone if you make yourself ill.

Support in Day to Day Activities

Most people with personality disorders can learn, over time, to live with their disorder. It may require a dependence on some medication to help alleviate stress and anxiety; it may also require them to follow a strict daily regime; which may appeal to those who have compulsive disorders!

In all these activities they will require support as they adjust and, ultimately, reduce their dependence on you. The level of support required will depend upon the severity of the condition and the stage of treatment but it is likely that the day to day requirements will remain high for some time before they gradually take charge of their own life again.

This will continue to be a drain on your time and it is essential to consider what help is available to stop you undertaking it all by yourself. There are many facilities in the community which will monitor and assist those who need it. At this stage of the process it will be easier for strangers to gain the trust of your loved one and assist them; giving you a much needed break.

At times it may even be necessary to indulge in some respite care; this should not be seen as a failure on your part. You must look after yourself first and foremost.

Chapter 5: How Does A Sociopath Affect Relationships?

Now that you can spot a sociopath, it's time you thought about the kind of relationship which they would have. Since one out of four people is a sociopath, it's not uncommon to find normal people dating sociopaths. The first thing you will notice is that a sociopath is a charming person. This often puts the victims in a good but false frame of mind. In the beginning, you will find that sociopaths can get away with anything. This is the reason why sociopaths are dangerous. They can be extremely witty and be the soul of any party. They are great talkers and seem guileless and innocent. You get carried away or sometimes swept off your feet by such people. All this time sociopaths are scheming and plotting to take advantage of you. They are ruthless and will use you to climb up the corporate ladder. They are social climbers and will manipulate you to get them the right contacts. You may be gullible enough to introduce them to influential people, only to realize later that this person has intentionally and selfishly misused your connections.

A sociopath is more likely to dump you after they squeeze whatever resources you can provide to them. People have been financially ruined by having relationship with a sociopath. They also lead to poor self-esteem in victims of their manipulation. Often, it is too late for the victims to save themselves. It's therefore essential to identify sociopaths by their sweet talking, manipulative behavior before they create havoc in your life. If you have noticed any unexplained loss of money from your wallet? Do you think someone is stealing from you? Has your credit card been swiped without informing you? If you have been in any of the above situations, it's time you started observing people around you. Sociopaths are glib liars and will certainly come up with creative excuses when they are caught. A sudden emergency may have compelled them to use your credit card. Maybe, they had to help someone in dire need and therefore took some cash from your wallet, but forgot to inform you. These are some excuses which you may be met with. You must look beyond the excuses and confirm the vents purportedly given by sociopaths. You will be surprised that all their excuses are lies.

Initially, a sociopath will sweep you off your feet. They will start behaving differently once they start getting closer to you. They have no normal emotions. They study the weaknesses of others, like a hunter studies his prey. They probably know more about your behavior and can anticipate your reaction in a given situation. They can also give you a cold shoulder if they realize that you cannot be of any help to them. Sometimes, you can get carried away by the charm of a sociopath to an extent that you refuse to believe others who warn you about his or her real persona. You can even commit yourself to a long tem relationship without realizing the consequences. It's advisable to listen to other voices especially if they are contrary to your own views. It can save you from trouble in future.

Chapter 6: Clues To Antisocial Behaviors

Childhood clues are often present in sociopaths and psychopaths as was previously referenced when mentioning PhD Kent Kiehl. Individuals who eventually have a diagnosis of antisocial personality disorder such as psychopath or sociopath have a pattern of behavior that begins in childhood. They typically violate the safety and rights of others, even basic ethical rights. They tend to break laws, rules, and societal norms. The key to spotting this behavior as an adult working with children or as a parent is to be receptive. Observing the actions and behaviors of children as they age will help parents and adults see if there is an issue that needs to be corrected or addressed.

There are problems with diagnosing a child with any antisocial personality disorder, mainly the child is still developing and bound to test certain morals, ethics, and societal norms. A repetitive pattern that meets the four categories of conduct disorder is used to determine if a child may develop sociopathic or psychopathic tendencies after they reach 18. The categories that meet conduct disorder include: an aggression towards animals and people, deceitfulness or theft, destruction of property and very serious rule violations.

Parents and adults who notice this behavior in children need to address the problem, seek a diagnosis and determine if there is an option to treat the child. Kiehl expresses a problem with treating patients who have psychopathic disorder in that the person can be deceitful, try to manipulate the situation, or become worse with treatment. However, not attempting to correct the behavior or assess the individuals properly is negligent.

Psychopaths and sociopaths are not all violent. Some have intelligence enough to rein in the impulse control and anger outburst in most situations. It can be difficult once a child reaches adulthood to see the clues particularly if they are smart and not a person you are around each day.

There are clinical methods for assessing both psychopaths and sociopaths. But most of us do not study psychology and may be unaware we are working right next to a person with a type of antisocial personality disorder. If you pay attention there are clues that will help you spot a psychopath or sociopath. One or more traits may be present and these traits may be low on a scale of 0 to 2, where 0 means it does not apply and 2 means it fully applies.

Before moving into the chapter on clinical assessment criteria there is one way you can assess a situation you may find yourself in. As there are clues in childhood that parents can watch for and attempt to get proper help, there are traits in adults that will show if they tend towards sociopathic or psychopathic behaviors. It is a combination of traits as outlined in the definitions. Often a highly intense person that is impulsive or easy to anger is one indication they may have an antisocial personality disorder. If this same person is charming and intelligent, while remaining withdrawn it is a clue to you that the person may be a sociopath or psychopath. Remember that the person can be withdrawn without seeming like it. Often they tell you information that is not true or they turn the conversation back to you if they are asked too personal a question.

The best clue to any sociopath or psychopath is the lies. While it can mean other personality disorders exist like schizophrenia, borderline, or narcissistic personality disorder if coupled with other traits like charisma and impulsivity you know there is a significant mental health issue. The lies told by a person with psychopathic or sociopathic tendencies is going to tell outrageous lies which can be fact checked. Things will be exaggerated, sound more like a story, and yet for some reason sound totally believable. If questioned about the lie they may defend it at all costs, become extremely angry, or try to win you over.

Another sign that you are dealing with a sociopath or psychopath is their intelligence. They are highly intelligent. There is no need to lie and they could attain an extremely high education; however, the desire to do so may be lacking. Given the combination of intelligence and lies they are able to spin many functioning sociopaths and psychopaths have held high positions in government. There are leaders of countries who have certainly fit the criteria to be discussed in the next chapter. They were even able to be violent without being seen as mentally ill because it was in the name of their country and defense of their country. Timur-e Lang is a good example of this situation. To restore the Mongol Empire he killed many with his army, taking everything the people had owned and turning some into slaves. Yet he had a following because he could charm, threaten and use his intelligence.

Chapter 7: Best Way To Disentangle From A Psychopath

You must be thinking: we said you just give the psychopath a cold shoulder – no phone calls, no text messages and no contact whatsoever. That was a suggestion, alright; and still is, where it works. But then, considering the psychopath's obsession with conquest, that method may just provide greater motivation to pursue you.

So, what method is likely to kill the psycho's drive?

Take the example of a normal person – normal as opposed to a psychopath, of course. When you are pursuing something and it takes long to get it and you are getting more and more tired, the reason you keep at it is that you can smell hope; you can see light at the end of the tunnel.

Now, that is the best principle to consider when getting set to drop a psychopath. Give the person little or no hope of succeeding with you. Make yourself unlikeable in terms of succumbing to the psychopath's manipulation. You are not giving the guy a cold shoulder alright, but you are not providing any satisfaction either.

I can imagine the boredom, for instance, if, after having a lengthy conversation the previous day on how useless your parents are you deliver your parents' warm regards, telling your psycho you are the one that called to know how they were doing. That is clearly, but with apparent innocence, a way of saying, it has not registered to me that my parents are useless and I have no intention of cutting ties with them.

But remember you paid attention to the psychopathic condemnation of your parents the previous day. So you did not provoke the psycho into violence by countering his or her stand – in the mind of your psycho, therefore, you are either naïve or possibly too stupid to try and sharpen. In due course, the attempts to alienate you from your folks will come to an end.

But the psychopath's desire to control someone is insatiable. What will happen then when you do not succumb?

Great question: the psycho will leave you alone and go looking for an easy prey. So, if it was a marriage you wanted to wind up, the opportunity presents itself in a smooth, non-violent way; just by not giving the psychopath the satisfaction of control and manipulation. Remember if you go the argument way, talking for one side and the psychopath for the other side, there is going to be drama; and that is the thrill that psychopaths thrive in.

Here, we are not groping in the dark. This is a scientifically tested method that goes in the name of Gray Rock Method.

Another way to apply Gray Rock

If your instincts tell you that someone leans towards the psychopathic, pretend to be dumb and boring right from the start when your paths cross. They will divert attention to more interesting people. In case they are relatives, just talk boring facts of the weather, who delivered a child when, how fast the city is growing, and so on. Psychopaths like to learn about you and your feelings; so avoid that zone and you deprive them of fodder.

Suppose meeting them is inevitable?

Well, in some cases, you cannot get rid of some psychopaths from your life, like in cases where you have children together. How the gray rock method helps in such instances is you pretending that you are not interested in the areas the psycho is trying to provoke you.

In fact, you can also be 'manipulative', that is, in a subtle way, by showing concern where it does not really matter. I'm imagining you putting emphasis on your psychopathic ex-partner coming on time to pick the kids during visitations. And considering the psycho would be glad to prove control over you, your kids will be picked late and you will be inwardly smiling; because in any case, the less time the kids have with the psychopath the happier you will be. Here, you are using the gray rock method selectively — showing interest here, ignoring there.

Chapter 8: Avoiding Manipulation In The Future

Experiencing a manipulative relationship is traumatic. Perhaps, if you're reading this book, there are a lot of negative emotions welling inside you, wanting to burst. No one is really at fault when you become trapped in a manipulative relationship, except the person who manipulates. Although your innate weakness is obviously antecedent to manipulation, you really cannot blame yourself for it, for we were created as we are. However, changing yourself for the better is not a bad idea, and it's actually recommended. More or less, the whole gist of this chapter can be summarized by this: "If you make a mistake once or twice, it's okay. You're not at fault. You can do better. However, if you repeatedly submerge yourself in the same situation, and not learn anything, then you don't have anyone to blame but yourself".

Aside from following the procedures discussed in the previous chapter, it is recommended that you fully arm yourself with knowledge acquired from your experiences, in order to become free from being a subject of manipulation as long as you live. These are some advice:

1. Beware of flatteries and charm, especially those coming from a complete stranger. Manipulators are masters of deceit. You won't always be ready and alert for them. Unfortunately, manipulators surround us whenever or wherever we are. In order to successfully sort them out from the rest, you have to be under the manipulative situation itself. Since you have been manipulated before,

you can more or less identify a pattern in manipulators hiding in sheep's clothing.

When you first meet a manipulator, in order to get into your trusting side, the first that they use is charm. He/She will give compliments to either stop or encourage you from doing something. More often than not, the wish of the manipulator is opposite to your own. This should raise your antennae, and alert your guard against possible manipulation.

However, it's not good to always be a judgmental, so you may allow yourself to find out the suspected person's next moves. If he/she uses silent treatment, regression (e.g. pouting, frowning or making a pained face) and reasoning to make you do what he/she demands of you, then most likely, you're dealing with a manipulative freak. The last gauge is coercion and debasement. At this stage, the manipulator is destroying your reputation, acting hostile or forceful, and resorting to physically and mentally abusive tactics. If you're lucky and knowledgeable enough, you won't allow yourself to be dragged into this situation. At the most, it's better to keep away from the person once he/she starts using the second set of tactics in manipulation.

2. Keep your ambitious self in check. The gain or loss of rewards in exchange to compliance is an effective control lever used time and again by seasoned manipulators. Pushing beyond your limits to get your goals or do something better is not bad. We all have ambitions, and life is too short to give up without finding out if you can do better than what you can right now. However, being greedy enough to sacrifice the things more valuable, like your happiness and your family' happiness, free mind and peaceful sleep every night, is an entirely different matter. Greed is a fuelling factor for both the

manipulator and the manipulated. Patience is a virtue. Be contented with what you have, and what you can do. There is always the right time for everything.

3. Always choose the righteous thing to do. There is no such thing as half-bad, or slightly illegal. It's still not the right thing to do. Your karma may come in a form of a person, who's ready to use your bad (hidden) records to manipulate or control you.

4. Find and remember who's who. There are manipulators, but there are also non-manipulative people. There are people who will try to persuade or influence you, but they truly have your best interests at heart.

Chapter 9: Step By Step Instructions To Handle Narcissistic Abuse

We're all equipped for misuse when we're baffled or harmed. We might be blameworthy of reprimanding, judging, retaining, and controlling, yet a few victimizers, including narcissists, take maltreatment to an alternate level. Narcissistic Abuse can be physical, mental, passionate, sexual, money related, and additionally otherworldly. A few sorts of psychological mistreatment are difficult to spot, including control. It can incorporate passionate coercion, utilizing dangers and terrorizing to practice control. Narcissists are experts of obnoxious attack and control. They can venture to such an extreme as to make you question your own recognitions, called gaslighting. The Motivation for Narcissistic Abuse

Recall that narcissistic character issue (NPD) and misuse exist on a continuum, going from quietness to brutality. Seldom will a narcissist assume liability for their conduct. For the most part, they deny their activities, and expand the maltreatment by accusing the person in question. Especially, threatening narcissists aren't annoyed by blame. They can be savage and enjoy perpetrating torment. They can be so serious and corrupt that they participate in hostile to social conduct. Try not to mistake narcissism for hostile to social character issue.

The target of narcissistic maltreatment is power. They act with the aim to decrease or even hurt others. The main thing to recollect about purposeful maltreatment is that it's intended to rule you. Victimizers will probably expand their control and authority, while making uncertainty, disgrace, and reliance in their casualties.

They need to feel better than maintain a strategic distance from shrouded sentiments of mediocrity. Understanding this can engage you. Like all harassers, notwithstanding their safeguards of anger, pomposity, and self-expansion, they experience the ill effects of disgrace. Seeming feeble and embarrassed is their greatest dread. Knowing this current, it's fundamental not to take actually the words and activities of a victimizer. This empowers you to defy narcissistic maltreatment.

Errors in Dealing with Abuse

At the point when you overlook a victimizer's intentions, you may normally respond in a portion of these insufficient ways:

1. Submission. On the off chance that you assuage to evade strife and outrage, it enables the victimizer, who considers it to

be shortcoming and an occasion to apply more control.

2. Arguing. This additionally shows shortcoming, which narcissists disdain in themselves as well as other people. They may respond contemptuously with scorn or sicken.

3. Withdrawal. This is a decent transitory strategy to gather your musings and feelings, yet isn't a viable procedure to manage misuse.

4. Contending and Fighting. Contending over the realities squanders your energy. Most victimizers aren't keen on current realities, yet just in supporting their position and being correct. Verbal contentions can rapidly raise to battles that channel and harm you. Nothing is picked up. You lose and can wind up feeling more defrauded, hurt, and sad.

5. Clarifying and Defending. Anything past an essentially forswearing of a bogus allegation leaves you open to more maltreatment. At the point when you address the substance of what is being said and clarify and shield your position, you support a victimizer's entitlement to pass judgment, endorse, or misuse you. Your response sends this message: "You have control over my confidence. You reserve the privilege to endorse or oppose me. You're qualified for be my appointed authority."

6. Looking for Understanding. This can drive your conduct in the event that you urgently need to be perceived. It depends on the bogus expectation that a narcissist is keen on getting you, while a narcissist is just keen on winning a contention and having the predominant position. Contingent on the level of narcissism, sharing your sentiments may likewise open you to more damage or control. It's

smarter to impart your emotions to somebody safe who thinks about them.

7. Reprimanding and Complaining. Despite the fact that they may act extreme, since victimizers are fundamentally uncertain, inside they're delicate. They can dish it, yet can't take it. Grumbling or reprimanding a victimizer can incite wrath and noxiousness.

8. Dangers. Causing dangers to can prompt reprisal or blowback on the off chance that you don't complete them. Never make a danger you're not prepared to implement. Limits with direct results are more compelling.

9. Refusal. Try not to fall into the snare of forswearing by pardoning, limiting, or justifying misuse. Furthermore, don't fantasize that it will disappear or improve at some future time. The more it goes on, the more it develops, and the more vulnerable you can turn into.

10. Self-Blame Don't reprimand yourself for a victimizer's activities and invest more energy to be awesome. This is a hallucination. You can't make anybody misuse you. You're just answerable for your own conduct. You will never be ideal enough for a victimizer to stop their conduct, which originates from their weaknesses not you.
 Defying Abuse Effectively

Permitting misuse harms your confidence. In this manner, it's critical to go up against it. That doesn't intend to battle and contend. It implies holding fast and supporting yourself unmistakably and tranquilly and having limits to secure your brain, feelings, and body. Before you set limits, you should:

1. Know Your Rights. You should feel qualified for be treated with deference and that you have explicit rights, for example, the privilege to your emotions,

the privilege not to have intercourse in the event that you decay, a privilege to protection, a privilege not to be shouted at, contacted, or slighted. In the event that you've been manhandled quite a while (or as a youngster), your confidence probably has been lessened. You may presently don't confide in yourself or have certainty.

2. Be Assertive. This takes learning and practice to try not to be detached or forceful. Attempt these momentary reactions to managing verbal putdowns:

*   I'll   consider   it.
* I'll never be the sufficient spouse (husband) that you sought after
* I don't care for it when you scrutinize me. It would be ideal if you stop." (Then leave)

* That's your assessment. I dissent, (or) I don't view it as such. * You're stating... " (Repeat information exchanged. Add, "Gracious, I see.")

* I won't to converse with you when you (depict misuse, for example "disparage me").

At   that   point   leave.
 * Agree to part that is valid. "Indeed, I consumed   the   supper."   Ignore
You're   a   spoiled   cook.
 * Humor - "You're adorable when you get irritated.

3. Be Strategic. Comprehend what you need explicitly, what the narcissist needs, what your cutoff points are, and where you have power in the relationship. You're managing somebody profoundly guarded with a character issue. There are explicit methodologies to having an effect.

4. Set Boundaries. Limits are decides that administer the manner in which you need to be dealt with. Individuals will treat you the manner in which you permit them to. You should recognize what your limits are before you can impart them. This implies

connecting with your emotions, tuning in to your body, knowing your privileges, and learning emphaticness. They should be express.

Try not to indicate or anticipate that individuals should guess what you might be thinking.

5. Have Consequences. Subsequent to defining limits, on the off chance that they're overlooked, it's essential to convey and conjure results. These are not dangers, but rather moves you make to secure yourself or address your issues.

6. Be Educative. Exploration shows that narcissists have neurological deficiencies that influence their relational responses. You're best methodology is to teach a narcissist like a youngster. Clarify the effect of their conduct and give motivators and support to various conduct. This may include conveying outcomes. It requires

arranging what you will say without being enthusiastic.

The Narcissist in the Workplace

To a narcissist-business, the individuals from his "staff" are Secondary Sources of Narcissistic Supply. Their job is to gather the flexibly (in human talk, recall functions that help the pompous mental self portrait of the narcissist) and to control the Narcissistic Supply of the narcissist during droughts (basically, to idolize, revere, appreciate, concur, give consideration and endorsement, etc or, at the end of the day, be a crowd of people). The staff (or should we say "stuff"?) should stay latent. The narcissist isn't keen on anything besides the most straightforward capacity of reflecting.
At the point when the mirror gets a character and an existence, the narcissist is angered. At the point when autonomous leaning, a worker may be at risk for being

sacked by his boss (a demonstration which exhibits the business' power).

The worker's assumption to be the business' equivalent (fellowship is conceivable just among approaches) harms the last narcissistically. The business is happy to acknowledge his workers as subordinates, whose very position serves to help his bombastic dreams. In any case, the affectedness lays on such delicate establishments, that any trace of equity, contradiction or need (that the narcissist "needs" companions, for example) compromises the narcissist significantly. The narcissist is really unreliable. It is anything but difficult to destabilize his extemporaneous "character". His responses are just in self-preservation.

Exemplary narcissistic conduct is when glorification is trailed by degrading. The downgrading demeanor creates because of contradictions OR just in light of the fact that time has disintegrated the representative's ability to fill in as a FRESH Source of Supply.

The representative, underestimated by the narcissistic business, gets sub-par as a wellspring of praise, reverence and consideration. The narcissist consistently looks for new excites and upgrades. The narcissist is infamous for his low limit of protection from weariness. His conduct is hasty and his history turbulent correctly due to his need to acquaint vulnerability and danger with what he sees as "stagnation" or "moderate demise" (i.e., schedule). Most associations in the working environment are essential for the groove - and consequently establish a token of this everyday practice - collapsing the narcissist's pretentious dreams.

Narcissists do numerous superfluous, off-base and even perilous things in quest for the adjustment of their swelled mental self view.

Narcissists feel choked by closeness, or by the steady tokens of the REAL, bare essential world. It lessens them, causes them to understand the Grandiosity Gap (between their mental self portrait and reality). It is a danger to the unsafe equilibrium of their character structures (generally "bogus", that is, created) and treated accordingly.

Narcissists everlastingly move the fault, shift responsibility elsewhere, and take part in intellectual disharmony. They "pathologise" the other, cultivate sentiments of blame and disgrace in her, disparage, degrade and mortify so as to safeguard their feeling of vainglory.

 Narcissists are neurotic liars. They don't consider anything it in light of the fact that their self is FALSE, a development. Here are a couple of valuable rules:

Never can't help contradicting the narcissist or negate him; Never offer him any closeness;

Look awed by whatever characteristic issues to him (for example: by his expert accomplishments or by his attractive features, or by his prosperity with ladies, etc);

Never help him to remember life out there and in the event that you do, associate it some way or another to his feeling of pretentiousness ("These are the BEST workmanship materials ANY work environment will have", "We get them EXCLUSIVELY", and so forth);

Try not to offer any remark, which may straightforwardly or in a roundabout way encroach on his mental self portrait, power, judgment, omniscience, aptitudes, capacities, proficient record, or even ubiquity. Awful sentences start with: "I think you disregarded ... committed an error here ... you don't have a clue ... do you know ... you were not here yesterday so ... you can't ... you ought to ... (seen as impolite burden, narcissists respond seriously to limitations put on their opportunity) ... I (never notice the way that you are a different, autonomous substance, narcissists see others as augmentations of their selves, their disguise measures were crashed and they didn't separate properly)..." You get its essence.

Could the narcissist be outfit? Will his energies be directed profitably?

This would be a profoundly defective - and even hazardous - "exhortation". Different administration masters indicate to show us how to outfit this power of nature known as dangerous or neurotic narcissism. Narcissists are driven, visionary, aggressive, energizing and profitable, says Michael Maccoby, for example. To disregard such an asset is a criminal waste. We should simply figure out how to "handle" them.

However, this solution is either gullible or pretentious. Narcissists can't be "took care of", or "oversaw", or "contained", or "directed". They are, by definition, unequipped for cooperation. They need compassion, are exploitative, desirous, haughty and feel entitled, regardless of whether such an inclination is similar just with their pretentious dreams. Narcissists disguise, plan, crush and fall to pieces. Their drive is enthusiastic, their vision seldom grounded in all actuality, their human relations a catastrophe. Over the long haul, there is no suffering advantage to hitting the dance floor with narcissists - just transient and, frequently, fraudulent, "accomplishments".

Chapter 10: The Psychopath Checklist

Back in the 1970's, a Canadian professor, Dr. Robert Hare developed a diagnostic tool for use in rating a person's tendencies towards psychopathic or antisocial behavior. Dr. Hare was a world-renowned researcher in criminal psychology, having spent 30 years studying the psychopath concept. The list he devised was partly based on work he carried out with inmates at a prison in Vancouver.

The list is called the PCL-R – Psychopathy Checklist – Revised – and is used in courtrooms and institutions to determine the potential risk that may be posed by individuals who are prisoners or in psychiatric units. This is because many psychopaths who offend once will go on to commit repeat offences, sexual assault and other violent crimes.

There are two parts to the PCL-R – an interview and a review of the file records and the history of the subject. There is a list of twenty symptoms on a rating scale that lets examiners who are fully qualified compare the psychopathic tendencies of the subject with a prototypical psychopath, through characteristics determined over the thirty years that Dr. Hare carried out his work. Each of the items is scored between 0 and 2 depending on how it applies to the individual – 0 means it doesn't apply, 1 means some degree of tendency and 2 is a full tendency to display the symptom. The test can only be considered as valid if it is carried out by a qualified and experienced clinician under the correct conditions. They symptoms on the list are:

Displays superficial, glib charm

Has an exaggerated estimation of self-worth

Has a need for stimulation

Is a pathological liar

Is cunning and manipulative

Shows no remorse or guilt over anything

Displays a superficial response to emotion

Is callous and shown no empathy

Lives a parasitical lifestyle

Has poor control of behavior

Is sexually promiscuous

Displayed behavioral problems from early in life

Has no realistic goals for the long-term

Is impulsive

Is irresponsible

Will not take any responsibility for his or her own actions

Will not settle in a long term marital relationships, may have been married several times

Will have a history of juvenile delinquency

Conditional release will have been revoked

Shows criminal versatility

Someone who receives a top score of 40 would be akin to a prototypical psychopath while someone who has no psychopathic tendencies whatsoever would have a score of zero.

Chapter 11: Sociopaths In Office And Corporate Corridors

These are their favorite haunts – power centers and corporate corridors. Studies have shown that there are more sociopaths up at the top of the ladder than at the bottom. Sociopaths are smart guys who look good in suits and ties. They are glib talkers and can charm people like no one else. However, they have the capacity to cause heavy damage to human resources.

Typically, sociopaths start off pretty well in an office setup. Slowly they start trying their tricks. They may try to isolate a single office hand and play him against others. Sociopaths like to watch the fun after putting the cat among the pigeons. The office atmosphere can quickly deteriorate under such circumstances. Your office will look like a war zone when you are up against a sociopath.

A typical sociopath will try to look busy and active while they try to palm off responsibility. If you happen to be the boss of a sociopath, it's better to lay down the rules beforehand and in writing. Sociopaths will try to wriggle off their responsibly. They will palm off the blame if anything goes wrong and hog the limelight if something were to go well. This is the typical trait of a sociopath.

If a sociopath happens to be your boss you might as well start praying. They are sadists at heart and will wring the life out of you. They will make you stay back way beyond working hours while they themselves will go for golf after lunch. They will be mean and callous to you. They simply don't care what you think of them. Don't expect to be praised by a sociopath.

They will never acknowledge your good work but shout at you on trivial issues. Sociopaths love to castigate their juniors in public. They like to humiliate and shame people. Sociopaths seldom stay in one work place for long. They like to hunt in fresh grounds.

If you happen to be the boss of a sociopath, you should prepare yourself to face a barrage of lies and bigger lies. They will never accept mistakes. They will always shift blame to someone else. They will look very busy and active but they are lazy and don't like to work. Sociopaths believe that they can charm anyone. Don't fall into their trap. Assign clear duties to them. Give them specific tasks. Ask for reports often. You will soon notice that they start avoiding you. You might even find a resignation letter, if you insist on results.

Despite all the negative traits of a sociopath, you will still find them at the top echelons of corporate world. This is attributed to their ability to climb up the ladder by whichever means. They will manipulate, steal and charm their way up. They are ruthless and this helps them immensely in certain professions where their negative traits are valued. They are glib talkers and lie without hesitation and without shame or remorse.

Chapter 12: What Should You Do?

Given the 30 million approximated psychopaths, sociopaths, and individuals with antisocial personality disorder it is very possible that you live near, work with, or have met someone with this behavioral disorder. Their symptoms or behavioral issues may have been mild, almost unrecognizable as an issue. But what should you do if you are working with someone that has more than a mild or "partial" behavioral disorder? What if more than 10 on the Hare list apply at level 2? Is there really something you can do to protect yourself and should you be overly concerned?

Becoming paranoid about who you meet and interact with on a daily basis is not going to do you any favors. Fearing to go out of the house because you may encounter a psychopath or sociopath is not really conducive to making a living and enjoying your life. Since we cannot all walk around in a safety bubble it is far better to understand the previous chapter as well as the differences that separate antisocial personality, sociopathic, and psychopathic disorders. If you can learn to recognize these behaviors you will be one step closer to protecting yourself should you find yourself face to face with a violent individual with conduct disorder issues.

Before breaking what you should do into different situations and talking about recognizing an approach there are some things you can do to protect yourself.

Be aware of your surrounding at all times. This is one of the hardest things for most people to do. We always have things on our minds whether it is driving, walking, going into a store, picking up the kids, or at work. We also have the thought that "it can't happen to us" until it happens. You do not have to alter the way you live, but you should follow some important steps.

• Look around you before you exit your car.

• If you have a garage keep the door closed until you are in your car and ready to leave.

• If you are leaving your home, apartment, place of work, or any other establishment look around, take note of anyone who seems to be alone or loitering.

• If you feel uncomfortable wait until several people are leaving before you step outside.

• When you leave work at night always leave with others. Two or three people should each go out and everyone should wait until each person is safely inside their cars.

• Before getting into your car check for broken windows and test that the car was locked. If all looks safe still shine a light into the backseat or if its daylight just look at the backseat.

• When leaving a place have your keys out, put the key between your index and middle finger for a quick jabbing motion if necessary.

• When you enter a restaurant or other building be conscious of where the exits are.

As long as you have an awareness of yourself and where you are, you can avoid most situations. If someone is dangerous and they are trying to harm you, there may be nothing you can do. However, being aware of everything around you helps you to have a better reaction time should something occur. You can still talk on the phone or text, but look up, look around, and make sure you are listening to things around you. Do not tune out the world because you have something on your mind.

Take self defense classes. Whether you are a man or a woman something could happen to you. Being prepared is essential to ensuring your safety. You may not be able to overpower someone, but you can defend yourself and learn how to handle a situation if you are in danger. One of the things about humans is that when prepared there is usually less panic. Panic might set in at first, but if you have gone through the motions of defense your brain can usually kick in to help rescue you. For example being taught how to actually break a taillight if you are stuck in a trunk is better than watching a video of someone else doing it.

Being proactive in self defense training and being aware are only ways to potentially help yourself in dangerous situations. You may never need it. You certainly do not need to get a carry permit for a concealed weapon unless this makes you more comfortable.

Recognizing an Approach

Recognizing an approach is very important. Most psychopaths who are violent tend to have a plan. They have singled out a specific individual. In a public place they are likely to look for someone who fits their criteria and who is alone. Often they are charming. They will have a good story that is believable. Yet, there will be something in the story that seems like a lie or you know is a lie. Only by being aware of yourself will it be easy for you to determine the lie. There are some noticeable signs that a person has an antisocial personality disorder. If you can learn to read those and understand those it will be easier to recognize an approach. Unless you know a person you should never go with them to a place you do not know alone.

Ruses can be used by those with violent tendencies. A killer will have a story that is meant to get you alone. It is not always the case and you should not think it will be something out of a Hollywood story—not that it can't be. The point is that sometimes horrific events do happen. For sociopaths it is more about the moment where an opportunity presents itself rather than a formed approach; however, this is again not always the case. By being prepared and knowing what is going on around you it is easier to protect yourself.

Dealing with Personal Antisocial Personality Disorder

There are a few warning signs that someone may be a psychopath or sociopath. Men and women can have one or the other antisocial personality disorder. This means someone you date or consider dating may fit this disorder category. To protect yourself understand some of the not so noticeable traits they might have.

First an individual with a history of occupational or financial instability may have this disorder. It is not always the case as other behavioral disorders can create an issue with financial stability too. As a sign it needs to be assessed with other characteristics. Often work or financial stability come with an overall disregard for the rules such as arriving late to work, sleeping on the job, stealing, and insubordination. Remember most have anger issues, which can lead to arguments with their coworkers and boss.

Individuals with antisocial personality disorder, as we have been discussing, lack emotional capabilities like love, empathy and remorse. Psychologists studying this disorder often find the individual tends to get serious way too quickly. It may be about an intimate relationship or after a first date saying that it is already love.

Negative behaviors will be present particularly if angered. When talking the person will have this viewpoint that the world owes him/her. They rarely tip, volunteer, or care about living in a clean world. Usually the individual will see amusement in other's suffering. This means strangers are treated badly. The person might mistreat an animal, handicapped person, or homeless person. It might be a viewpoint or something they say, but it can also be something you see with regards to treating strangers horribly.

A last and more difficult trait to see is that the person is usually never wrong, even when they are. They will become angry if argued with or told they are wrong. Inappropriate or lame excuses for an error are often the first signs that the person has an antisocial personality disorder.

If you find that you are around someone like this already, but have not been harmed in any way they are probably on the lower scale of psychopathic or sociopathic tendencies. It does not mean they couldn't turn violent or are not difficult to be around.

It is often best not to incite their anger as much as possible. If the person wants to engage their anger you can step back, take time to cool off, and decide if you want to avoid the person or continue dealing with their behavior. It is always better not to point out errors or things that will make the person angry in order to avoid a confrontation. If you ever feel you are in danger you definitely need to leave, seek the police and make a report about what happened. Sometimes the only way for a person with antisocial personality disorder characteristics to get help is to make a report.

Handling Workplace Antisocial Personality Disorder

Psychologists break down people with antisocial personality disorder in the workplace by the type of position they may be able to hold. Remember many psychopaths can be highly functioning. Even sociopaths can be for a short period of time. Executives, corporate, business, successful, office, white collar, organizational, occupational, and industrial are some of the headings provided to categorize psychopaths in the workplace. Studies indicate about 3 to 4% of individuals in senior positions have psychopathic characteristics. Even though the percentage seems small it is still possible for the person to do extreme damage to the company or the people working for the company.

There are ten positions that seem to attract psychopaths more than others: CEO, lawyer, salesperson, media, surgeon, police officer, journalist, clergyperson, civil servant, and chef. In the workplace you are still going to see the behavioral patterns you would see with a personal encounter with a psychopath or sociopath. However, in the workplace it might seem more acceptable.

Typically there is public humiliation of others particularly if the psychopath knows there was a mistake made by that person or if they just want to be amused. Spreading gossip through the form of malicious lies without any remorse or guilt when asked about their behavior is a pattern. An individual in the workplace will typically go from manipulation to causing high anxiety in order to be amused or get what they desire.

There is an extremely long list of other characteristics psychopaths in the workplace can have. They usually sabotage, refuse to take responsibility, and have unrealistic goals for employees or themselves. They can choose "victims" to constantly pick on in the workplace for sheer amusement. It is not violence in all cases, but more of a mental game that can cause harm to the one receiving the treatment.

The one thing that keeps getting psychopaths hired at various workplaces, particularly in the corporate world is they make a charming first impression. They are positive, goal oriented, and able to hide their anger from most recruiters. While subtle body language and micro expressions may be present, most people are unable to read the more subtle signs. It also helps that many psychopaths are accomplished liars. Sociopaths to a certain degree can also gain high employment positions, but their impulsivity typically makes this last a very short time. Of course the degree with which the person suffers from behavioral disorders will determine how easy or difficult it is to maintain a normal working life.

Like dealing with psychopaths and other behavior disorders in your personal life it is important that you know when to seek help. If you feel someone in a higher position is verbally abusive then you must report it. The more reports that are made the easier it will be for the company to see there is a distinct issue with a particularly employee no matter their charming behavior.

Chapter 13: Take Psychopath's Power Away With Understanding

"I'm an 'intelligent' sociopath. I don't have problems with drugs, I don't commit crimes, I don't take pleasure in hurting people, and I don't typically have relationship problems..."

— M. E. Thomas, Confessions of a Sociopath: A Life Spent Hiding in Plain Sight

Understanding psychopathy will give you an insight into all the painful ways in which the predator is living isolated and lonely. When you come to understand that they targeted you for their own desperation and not your 'flaws', you will take away their power over you. In this chapter, we'll delve a bit deeper into how you can set yourself free of a psychopath by understanding them.

Give Them the Benefit of the Doubt: Are They All the Same?

Only a small percentage of psychopaths become violent criminals. Most often, this happens due to additional damage to their minds caused by a traumatic and painful childhood. Understanding that not all psychopaths are the same will help you alleviate some of the fears and start to look at them from another perspective. The better you understand predatory personalities, the less power they have over you.

Not all of them are violent

Just because someone is a psychopath, that doesn't automatically make them violent. There are numerous types of psychopathy, and high-functioning ones tend to be well-balanced. The degree to which a psychopath is prone to violence depends on their ability to regulate anger, which they often use to cloak fears and insecurities. If you're dealing with a psychopath who is more self-aware, they won't act aggressively. Violence doesn't serve any purpose to them.

Not all of them are antisocial

In general, psychopaths don't care for society and the rules in the same way most of us do. They don't have an emotional relationship with the society, but that doesn't mean that they don't understand the utility of the rules. A psychopath may not appreciate the concept of fairness, justice, or equality, but they do understand the reasoning behind the rules. Rules and laws create a peaceful living environment for everyone, including them. The psychopaths who understand the reasoning behind the law are usually not against it.

Not all of them are toxic

Psychopaths who tend to act manipulative and toxic usually do so to defend themselves from their own trauma and feelings of helplessness and inadequacy. If a person came from a history of normal upbringing, and they are more self-aware than average, they won't feel the need to put down others to feel superior.

What is the main point of understanding psychopaths?

When you understand that not all psychopaths are the same, you'll understand that a predator is a type of a person who needs to feel superior to other people in order to compensate for their own trauma and insecurity. Your predator is a traumatized, troubled individual who needs to be in command of people to feel important. It is a trait specific to them, which sets them apart not only from most people, but also other psychopaths. By understanding their insecurities, it will be easier for you to break out of their influence.

Understand Their Emotional Disability

Removing the abuser from your headspace is essential to recover from psychopathic heartbreak and the damage they've caused you. You might feel hurt, and you feel like you want to get justice and closure. Ultimately, healing is a process you do with yourself. It is a self-led process.

Acknowledge their inability to care

The reason you won't be able to get closure, or any type of emotional satisfaction from a psychopath is that they don't care. For a person to say that they are sorry, it takes actually being sorry. While not all psychopaths are necessarily abusers, you can't really count on them to care about the damage that they've caused you. For this reason, taking the power away from a psychopath is something that is done within you.

Remove the predator from your head space

You can't take power away from a psychopath by confronting or arguing with them. Best case scenario, you can end up beating them down with arguments or scaring them away. But the damage that they've caused won't go away after they pack their bags. Their toxic influence is now inside your mind. Once you've broken up with a person and they've left your life, their influence had stopped. Now, the image in your mind of the other person is solely a reflection of your self-criticism.

If you're still haunted by the criticism and insults from the previous relationship, it is crucial for you to remove the predator from your mental space. How do you do that? The first thing is to stop trying to heal by trying to beat down the psychopath. This is impossible because of their low functioning limbic system. The genetic background of the illness doesn't allow them to change or feel remorse for the things that they've done. Essentially, you can't take them down because they don't care.

What you can do instead is to focus on self-healing. Learning about psychopathy will help you understand why the abusers actions resulted from their illness, and not your personal flaws.

Use their toxicity to learn about your value

Learning about your own value compared to the psychopathic disability will help you step out of feeling powerless and step into a headspace of empowerment. This will enable you to grow your own health, authority, power, money, and status. More importantly, you will start to regain spiritual peace. The reason that the psychopath still has a mental impact on you is because their actions and words are appealing to your insecurities, and understanding how severe disorder psychopathy is compared to your 'flaws' will show you that your 'flaws' are actually gifts.

Why psychopathy is a disability

One of the ways for you to heal from a psychopath is to understand their disorder. It will help you to understand their mind. By studying psychopathy you will understand why the person has treated you the way they have. To start off, you can understand that from the moment they were born their brain was different than that of ordinary people. An average person uses emotions to navigate their thoughts and regulate actions.

Thoughts come before emotions and emotions serve as a GPS for behaviors. Even in healthy people, all emotions are learned. You learned what is supposed to make you happy, sad, happy, fulfilled, or guilty. This results from a healthy cognitive process. A psychopath doesn't have that tool. Instead, their brain is capable of feeling certain negative emotions but hardly ever positive. For this reason, a psychopath doesn't get any gratification aside from fame, and praise. A psychopath doesn't get any emotional satisfaction from acting selflessly in any way.

Understanding this, you realize that the person did the things they did because they are unable to be happy. For a person to do good, they must be able to feel rewarded, and that reward comes in emotional fulfillment. Psychopaths are unable to be happy by making another person happy. The closest thing they come to happiness is the sense of gratification that they get through personal satisfaction. Moreover, psychopaths are deeply hurt and isolated by their inability to create connections. Even psychopathic killers are open to talk about feeling detached from the world, how that scares them and how lonely they feel.

How compassion for a psychopath helps you heal

While you may not be able to count on the psychopath to feel compassion for you, finding that place within you that has the strength to feel compassionate about them will help you heal. Understand that the person who hurt you suffers great emotional pain.

- They suffer because they are unable to connect.

- They suffer because they don't care about things that normal people care about.

- They feel isolated and detached and that scares them.

- The only thing that they are truly capable of feeling is personal gratification.

- They are angry at the world and feel like the world is against them because they can't fit in.

The world cares for a sensitive person, not for a person who lacks the ability and desire to connect. Knowing what a person who doesn't have the same morality as we do, can do to another person makes you probably value good people even more.

Acknowledge Psychopath's Spiritual Purpose

Psychopathy reminds us that altruistic morality is a choice. Deep down, most people are profoundly selfish in their mental structure. A person's mental structure evolves and grows around what's good for them. However, when you have emotions you have an unconscious knowledge that what benefits other people benefits you as well.

The only reason because another person is unable to just approach you, steal from you, or attack you is because it's illegal. It is because humanity has reached the consensus that there are certain limits to our behavior that we want to self-impose to live in a safe and compassionate environment.

Next, psychopathy reminds us of the importance of selflessness. Selflessness is also a choice. People are in no way obliged to be selfless. No one can force them to do it. Still, the reason why, if you go to surgery or end up in a hospital, you can receive a blood transfusion, which can save your life, is because there are so many people who are willing to give their blood. The reason why people with failing organs are able to get an organ transplant is because there are selfless people out there who are willing to donate organs.

Psychopathy reminds us of the importance of altruism and selflessness. Now, with the damage that the psychopathy has caused in your life, you are more aware of how important and how wonderful it is to be altruistic. You will appreciate kind and good people even more. This insight helps you get into a head space of gratitude. Knowing just how many good people are out there compared to the predators can serve as a base for you to start trusting again and begin to open up to love.

Chapter 14: The Art Of Apologising

Why apologising is important?

Because it shows:

Accountability.

You are able to take responsibility for your own actions.

Reality check.

No one is infallible, and you accept that.

Balance.

You don't put it all on the other person, you carry some too.

Willingness to improve.

Admittance of one's wrongs is the first step to recovery.

Opportunity to progress.

Once that's out of the way, you can both move on to figure out how to fix it, rather than spending any more time in a pointless blame game.

That is why apologies should be a common practice. Always beware of people who does not apologise, because you might be getting yourself into a road of pain.

Remember that if this person cannot admit wrong, you will be picking up the pieces on your own every time.

And now that we are clear on why apologising is important, let's talk about how to apologise.

Have you ever heard of Flash Fiction, or Nonfiction? It's a style of writing where you tell a complete story containing Plot, Conflict, and Resolution, in the shortest way possible. Here is an example:

I always find that one-liners tell the best stories.

As you can see, the story that I am telling in a flash is that apologies do not need the three devils, which are: *Buts*, *scapegoats* and *excuses*.

They do not. A simple *Sorry* is worth much more than a hundred excuses.

A *Sorry* without blaming others is just classy.

And the only *but* that you should ever care about is the acknowledgement that we all are human and make mistakes. Even you.

You can spend hours and hours explaining how you got into doing a mistake, but the reality is that, whatever the situation, we make mistakes because we are flawed, and that is the gist of it.

As a rule, **Less is More**, so just take it and move on.

Example:

'Did you get the kids?'

'Sh*t I forgot! Call them, I'm on my way', twenty minutes later, 'guys I'm so sorry, I hope you are OK.'

And that's OK, because we all make mistakes at some point or other...

Bad Example:

'Did you get the kids?'

'What?! You never told me I had to. Now what am I supposed to do, drive all the way there? For crying out loud, you're always dumping all sorts of sh*t on me—'

'They're your kids too, you know??'

And the argument goes on for days to end...

As we explained in the previous chapter, Reliability is very important, but we mustn't forget that we can't be expected to be 100% functioning 24/7, 365 days a year. It's just not realistic. We will make mistakes.

And when we do, we have two choices:

Being accountable and *Take it like a man*, so to speak, which means simply accept it and get on with it.

Create more unnecessary problems, cause chaos and discomfort for everyone, and ensure that we are not wanted around for a number of hours, or even days, for having made such a huge deal out of something that could, and should, have been sorted straight away without a fuss.

So how do apologies work, then?

Apologies should act as the glue between reliable and accountable, so that when things do go wrong (and they will) we get to keep the trust on us intact still.

An apology with an argument, a scapegoat, a position of inaction to prove a point, is as useful as a chocolate teapot.

Apologies need to be a step in between, not a final step. A change is needed. A fix is in order.

When an apology is used simply to stop an argument, the argument will never stop because the apology is meaningless without actions to follow.

Again, without proactivity, an apology is like an empty promise, a demonstration of annoyance, a useless label to get rid of you bringing the issue.

So, take care of your apologies, make sure that they mean something, don't waste precious time in excuses, blames, buts and other arguments. And accept no less from your partner.

In fact, use this new knowledge to ensure that you are in a loving relationship, and not a war of attire.

Always bear in mind that if one of you can never apologise without creating an argument, you are in the wrong relationship.

Chapter 15: How to Find a Sociopath in Three Steps

It doesn't matter if you're trying to identify a school shooter, a dangerous romantic partner, a fraudster online, or someone trying to steal your business, knowing the signs of sociopaths can help you. Sociopaths may have dangerous and hidden personality functions.

DSM-5 lists 10 criteria to identify antisocial character disorder1 or ASPD. However, it assumes that you have professional training as well as a lot information about the people. I won't teach you how to recognize ASPD, nor how to distinguish them from sociopaths (or psychopaths) or scam artists.

This section focuses on some of the hints they might give you in your first encounter or subsequent encounters. These tips could help you keep your distance from any tempting offers, no matter how appealing they may seem. Do not be a target.

The Theme of Dominance

According to the DSM-5, the most important characteristic of sociopaths is their inability to respect or violate the rights and freedoms of others. My experience over 30 years of dealing with legal cases, family disputes and work environment disputes as a high conflict expert has shown that the driving force behind sociopaths is their desire to dominate others. It may involve breaking the law. To dominate others, they want their possessions, money, partners, houses and cars, as well as their credibility. They also enjoy dominating other people for the thrill of it - the power and control they feel. Sociopaths don't have a conscience and will do whatever it takes to get what they want.

To quickly determine if someone has sociopathic characteristics (or any high conflict character pattern), I recommend using the three-step process I call The Web Method. It involves their WORDS, their EMOTIONS, and their BEHAVIOR. This includes actions that 90% of people would never do. These are some tips that you can pick up on a person using this approach.

Their words

Sociopaths are quick talkers. They are often utterly false in their words. They use many, many words to disguise their behavior. They might be completely different from what they claim to be. Be wary of extremes: big promises, big stories about the past and the future, big plans with no foundation or experience in what they are planning.

Positive words: You are the best! You are the reason I live! You will never be hurt! You deserve better! You are a better person than I am! You'll make us rich! You are the most amazing [wise, convincing and truthful], ethical, spiritual, and so forth. You are the most amazing person I have ever met. You can travel anywhere in the world with me! I will introduce you to well-known people! Believe me!

They can use incredibly negative words. On the other side, they may say very negative things after they have understood you. They will accuse you (their Target Of Blame) of small or nonexistent offenses. (Even though you did not lie to me and they lie all the time to you. You are the worst person I have ever met! You will never be hired! You will never be wanted by anyone! You are mine! I'll damage you! You won't be able to tell anyone what we are doing. After what you did, you deserve to be punished!

This is your right! You have done me a disservice, even though I have never hurt your feelings.

They make a switch: Sociopaths will often change between extreme charm or extreme threats to get what their heart desires, depending on what is working and what isn't. Be aware of strong opinions that they may abandon to take the opposite view when it is more practical. They will use any words that they feel help them dominate the situation at the moment. It's like an artist's palette.

They will also discover your weaknesses and vulnerabilities. They might use them to your advantage, and with words that will improve your ego. You'll be extraordinary successful. We have it all, thanks to your brains and my connections. They might even use your deepest fears. Your body isn't attractive. You will never be able to have intimate relationships with anyone. Or, nobody will ever hire or be intimate with you. You will never find a better person than me. You should be thankful... truly grateful.

Feelings

How do you feel about the person? Your emotions are often what tell you to be cautious. Many people marry sociopaths. They work with them, manage them or select them for responsible jobs. However, they often noticed warning signs. They preferred to believe what the person said, rather than paying more attention to their feelings. You should trust your feelings more than what they say. You should seek professional help if you feel uneasy or have a severe feeling. Ask around and do some research to find out what others think about so-and-so.

Fear: Sociopaths can be a threat to your safety. Sociopaths are predators and you may feel uncomfortable around them. It is possible to suddenly feel the need to escape a situation. Ask questions later. Do not let them make you feel ashamed. You can take your time to learn more about them.

Infatuation: This is the opposite extreme. People can easily fall for them because of their positive words. This is especially true if they are lonely, grieving, or lacking self-confidence. Megan Hunter co-authored my book Dating Radar. This is also true for hiring. Sociopaths can seem like superstars in today's competitive and hectic service industry. Sociopaths can make you feel like you are being swept away by potential company partners, workers, or companies. They are all around you so you need to keep your skepticism up no matter where you may be.

Extreme compassion: You may feel extremely compassionate towards someone. Sociopaths can tell great stories about being victims, and are skilled at claiming they have been there. They often exploit people who are vulnerable or in supportive situations, such as the elderly, victims of natural disasters, churchgoers, volunteers, etc. They may be able get you to give things that you would not normally do for anyone else by playing on your compassion.

Their conduct (The 90% Rule).

It is very easy to spot a sociopath by focusing on their behavior and not their words. Pay special attention to extreme behavior -- things that they do in a way 90% of people wouldn't. Ask yourself: Would I ever do this? Sociopaths are known for their severe conduct, but they quickly make excuses. I was stressed. He (or she) made me do it. It was necessary to do so given the actions of the other person. It doesn't matter what their conduct was, their excuses are often the same. They don't apologize and are never held responsible.

Targets for blame: Sociopaths often focus on the Targets of Blame, people they feel justified treating cruelly in their family, work or community. They often enjoy the suffering of others. They may be able to target anyone but many people will stay away from them. They will continue to target or bully the people they are trying to get rid of. They can either get angry at the sociopath, who is more aggressive than anyone else, or they can show their frustration or fear. Both of these approaches are foolish. It is better to calmly and peacefully break off than to let them affect your feelings. They'll enjoy your powerless anger,/or your powerless frustration. It just proves that they are dominating you.

Smiles, smirks and laughter: It is surprising to see how people enjoy the pain and hardship of others. Sociopaths can smile, laugh, or even smirk when victims tell their stories in court or depositions. This grabs your attention because 90% of people wouldn't do it. They would be able to see the victim's pain and feel empathy. You could see a sociopath if you observe someone smiling, laughing, or making jokes about another person's pain.

Youth conduct history: The DSM-5 requirement for antisocial personality disorder (sociopathic) is that the person has symptoms of the disorder by the age of 15. This could be a pattern of lying or torturing animals and pets, taking from relatives and complete strangers, starting fires, or other such behaviors. Sociopaths are known to do this quite often. They may attempt to cover up or make excuses. According to Florida's Parkland school shooter, the Parkland gunman had a history of causing harm to animals. Although many people were aware of this, they may not have understood the implications.

Chapter 16: Children And Sociopath Behavior

Along with worrying about whether or not you're dating a sociopath, or if your best friend is a sociopath, the worst fear is having a child who is a sociopath. We are all nervous parents. Nervousness and worry come naturally when we have children. It's part of being a parent, we stop worrying so much about ourselves and have constant fears regarding our children. Am I a good parent? Is my child going to be successful? Will my child turn out ok and be a happy adult? These are all questions that we, as parents find ourselves asking. Well, one question we may also ask ourselves if certain signs are present is, "Is my child a sociopath?" Now, before you start completely freaking out about this, and before you diagnose your child and rush him to a therapist, it's important to identify the actual signs of sociopath behaviors in children. As parents, we often want to immediately start thinking of the worst possible situation. That being said, children will experience many different things throughout their lives that will cause them to misbehave or act out in unusual ways. It's when the unusual behavior becomes the norm when it becomes an actual problem and something that should probably be looked into.

Learning how to effectively communicate with your child is incredibly important. Communicating effectively helps you learn about your child's needs and it helps them let you know what they need from you as well. Finding this communication is crucial. If you aren't doing a good job of communicating with your child, you may find yourself questioning whether or not your child is showing signs of sociopathic behavior or if they are just trying to get your attention. While communicating with your child at an early age is very important, as they get older it becomes even more essential. Communicating effectively is something that requires time and patience. You want to make sure you're communicating with them and letting them know what they're doing right and what they need to work on. If they're lying and not being truthful, instead of categorizing them as a sociopath immediately, try letting your child know why this is wrong and see if this helps the situation. Often times when children are showing signs of disruptive behavior, they can be eliminated by simply giving your child the attention they need and by communicating with them effectively. If your child is doing something wrong, let them know. Do not however tell them they are being "bad". Instead of using the word "bad" try using other words and giving your child positive examples of how they can change their disruptive behavior and why they need to. When you explain something to a child, it often becomes clearer. If your child grows up thinking they are bad, they will often continue these thoughts throughout their lives. Letting them know that what they did wasn't nice is important and it's a more effective way of getting your child to do what you want. Children are not bad, they simply need to be taught what's right and what's wrong. Setting rules at a very early age and encouraging children to understand that adults set the rules and children understand and accept them is important. We may think our child is showing signs of sociopathic behavior but when we start setting rules for our children and applying reinforcements, these behaviors are often eliminated.

Now, lying and manipulative behavior is something that definitely needs to be addressed with children, aggressive behavior however is far more serious. One of the most common signs of sociopathic behavior in children is their aggressive behavior. Aggressive behavior can be difficult for a parent to deal with. The type of aggressive behaviors that are present in children who may be sociopaths is different than general hitting, kicking, biting, and other forms of aggressive and physical behaviors. Often times, children with sociopathic behaviors tend to hurt animals. Hurting animals is a very common practice for these children. Causing animals pain is a practice for children with these behaviors because they take satisfaction in seeing an animal go through pain or even die. Just like adults with this disorder, children too get satisfaction over tricks and causing pain amongst others. This type of behavior can begin at a very early age and get much worse as the child gets older. For example, children with this disorder may start out by doing small things like hurting their toys or trying to cause things around them pain. As the child gets older, he may move on to other things like hurting the family dog, lighting things on fire and doing things to purposely trick his parents in a hurtful way. When a child enters into young adulthood he may move on to doing things such as hurting their friends, doing things at school to purposely hurt and sabotage others, or he may even try and convince others to follow them in their group and do negative and hurtful things to others. Other types of actions that children may show when they are sociopaths are stealing, breaking into homes, purposely trying to sabotage and hurt their siblings and parents or lying in order to get someone else in trouble. Maybe this person will break into their neighbor's house, steal something and then place this item in their sibling's room in order to get their sibling in trouble. Sociopaths get satisfaction over causing others pain, they do not care how the other victim feels pain as long as it occurs.

Disruptive behavior is another form of behavior that is often one of the first signs that becomes noticeable when parents begin to question whether or not there is a problem with their child. Disruptive behavior can be anything from swearing, bullying, bad language, lying and other negative forms of behavior that are often frowned upon by others. When a child exhibits this kind of behavior it may be normal. Many children will find themselves making mistakes and doing things once or twice that will not necessary turn them into a sociopath. Some of these negative behaviors listed above are completely normal. Now, remember that most children will experience a few of these behaviors often throughout childhood, it's when these behaviors become consistent that it becomes a problem. If you notice that your child is constantly in the principal's office due to bullying situations, and they're the bully, sit them down and find out what's wrong. Most of the time, the bully has actually been bullied themselves and they react by bulling others. Work with your child's teacher, principal, afterschool provider and anyone else in your child's life to identify the problem and cut it off at the pass before the problem gets worse. If you've done everything in your power to eliminate the negative behavior and you find that it's getting worse, you may want to discuss the child's behaviors with a doctor. These negative and disruptive behaviors may be linked to sociopathic behaviors and you may be able to eliminate these behaviors or at least prevent them from getting worse if caught at an early age. Do not let these behaviors go and do not categorize them as kids being kids. When your child is doing things to hurt others consistently, or if they are playing serious "pranks" on others that ultimately affect others' lives, consult with your doctor as your child may be showing signs of sociopathic behaviors.

Chapter 17: Healing From Psychopathic Abuse

Do you know that living with a crazy person can drive you crazy? The psychopath leaves you feeling low and unsure of yourself. You actually do not find much to be happy about in whatever environment you are in. Above all, you could become extremely distrusting.

What other negatives does the psychopath leave with you?

You get extremely irritated without much provocation

Your feeling of vulnerability is high

Disturbing thoughts keep nagging you

You experience unexplained fear and anxiety

Your self esteem is eroded

You may even feel physically unwell

You tend to be withdrawn

That inconclusive list goes to show that it is difficult for you to get your normal life back all on your own.

Why the emphasis on professional help?

You need assistance from a professional and some patience.

A professional will help you with your cognitive dissonance.

And what is that? Well, it is the psychological sort of denial; actually a defense mechanism that you develop when you get entangled with a psychopath. This denial is a way of keeping yourself numb from the reality that you are, or were, in a mess that you least expected. But the only way you can heal is by dealing with that unsavory truth and the pain that comes with it.

As long as you remain in denial, you will always have two voices ringing in your mind: one acknowledging that the psychopath is doing everything to disorient you, and another one assuring you that the psychopath actually has your interest at heart. So you will not be able to make a stand and move on.

Stay with people who empathize with your situation

You need to surround yourself with people who understand what you have experienced, and people who sincerely care about you. That way, you can ventilate without fearing that the people will judge you.

Open up to new friends

New company will help you get your mind off the unpleasant experience you had with the psycho. If you keep thinking about the bad experiences of the past, it can have the impact of retaining the past hurt and inhibiting your progress to healing.

Hobbies

Resume any hobbies you may have given up during the time you lived with the psychopath. Obviously, with the manipulating controlling nature of a psychopathic partner, it is unlikely you were able to pursue your hobbies as you would have wished.

Reach out to new opportunities

Take on a job or a new hobby that gets you inspired. All the new things you take up will help you have a different routine from what you had, and also get you exposed to people with a different and healthy mindset.

Why all the new things and keeping busy?

The reality is that unless you deal with the past pain and focus on other positive endeavors, there is the danger of:

Being a slave and a prisoner of your past bad experiences, always feeling the pain like it was still fresh and current

Developing pronounced negative characteristics, like looking at everybody with suspicion. If you keep mistrusting people who have your welfare in mind, you will be depriving yourself of healing and happiness.

Letting valuable time pass you by without doing things that you love.

Generally speaking, after you have parted ways with the psychopath, you need to do everything to replace the negative feelings from the past with positive ones that come with a promising and happy future. That way, you will not resort to blaming other people for your unhappiness the way the psychopath did to you.

Chapter 18: How To Handle A Psychopath

Most psychopaths move through life without getting detected. Since they are charismatic, smart, winners and very suave, distinguishing them from normal people is hard enough. However, if you finally detect someone as being a psychopath, these are the things to do;

Stop any more contact with them. This is not easy especially for someone who was romantically involved, but the sooner, the better. Ensure all links are severed to curtail any interaction or communication.

Keep a low profile. They have a tendency to be violent or murderous. Once you have severed all links, keep out of their sights. Be very cautious and there is no need to alert many others because word might get back to him/her and this could be disastrous. They are known to turn tables on people they pretended to love. There is no need for confronting them with the truth. Just keep out of their way.

Get back up. Since they have a tendency to be violent, they may not accept to let go so easily. Soliciting help from neighbors may backfire as well as they can spread falsehoods among your friends to get them on his or her side.

Get armed to protect yourself- Keep all your property and emotions out of their reach. Go a step ahead to inform your boss about it so that in case he/she turns up to soil your name, you are prepared.

Be strong. Showing signs of fear gets them excited. Be steady as you get back your life on course. Do not allow yourself to be intimidated. They may try to get you to communicate, but remain mute. Keep a good posture as you smile all through the mess.

Get prepared for the worst. They could stalk you, attack you via social media or through your former friends. Be prepared and do not get even. Instead, remain solid as a rock because the wave will slowly pass.

Forgive yourself. Do not blame yourself for having been involved with a psycho. They appear like any normal person and may therefore fool anyone. Be willing to forgive yourself as you move on with your life.

Move on. After accepting it happened, move on by being careful not to fall in the same ugly pit again. Psychos can make someone's life terrible, but you have learnt how to get them as far away from your life as possible.

Chapter 19: Schizophrenic Sam

There is something definitely wrong about your neighbor Sam. She argues that she hears people telling her that you should not be parking on the road, and they won't let her sleep unless you move your car elsewhere. She also swears that you are being followed by spirits, because an angel told her that you are a descendant of the 6th King of the Ancient Aztecs, and because of that status, you should know how to act according to the traditions. By traditions, she means that you should not be driving a Toyota, but a Mazda — specifically an apple green Mazda, which according to Sam, is prescribed by your ancestor himself.

What Is Schizophrenia?

Schizophrenia is a disorder that displays the symptoms that you notice in Sam, which involves hearing and seeing things that are not real, thus making you feel that people like Sam must have a hard time getting along with other people. Contrary to popular belief, it is not a dissociative identity disorder like multiple personality disorder. While a person with multiple personality disorder may also hear voices, he hears these voices as a part of his self, as if he is talking to other aspects of himself or other existing personas.

What makes it rather difficult to deal with people who are suffering from schizophrenia is that it is hard to establish to them that they are experiencing things that are far from real. That is because their minds operate differently and of course, they are experiencing illusions and hallucinations that they think are very valid and real because they see and hear them.

How To Deal With Schizophrenics

When you are dealing with people who have an altered sense of perception, you have to keep in mind that you are still dealing with regular people, except that they have a different sense of perception. It is not their fault that what they see and hear is different from yours, and there is no use in telling them that your reality is more valid than theirs. Schizophrenics, as well as people with multiple personality disorders, can be very intelligent and creative people, and may even be capable of living very successful lives.

If you have to communicate with these people, keep in mind that it is possible for them to be easily surprised — remember that they are also seeing and hearing other things that you may not be aware of. It would be best to talk to them slowly in order to notice and hear you better.

While schizophrenics and people with multiple personality disorder are not considered to be dangerous, it may be a good idea to have one of his family member with you. A physician may ask family members to talk to a therapist, who will teach family members coping strategies. Family members may also learn how to make sure a loved one knows how to stay on the medication and continue with treatment. Schizophrenics and those with multiple personality disorder may be extremely paranoid and careful with their surroundings. Moreover, it would be wise to know what types of moods they would normally have, or if they have a history of hostility. If possible, you may want to ask what kinds of "personalities" they normally deal with — the behavior of these people are widely affected by the illusions that they have, and knowing these illusions would help you communicate with and understand these people better.

Chapter 20: Questions To Ask Yourself If You Are A Sociopath

Now that you know how you can find out and recognize a sociopath, it is time to find out if you are a sociopath yourself. Maybe you have been having paranoia for quite some time now and you are afraid that you may be a sociopath, or maybe you have no clue that you are but never really had the chance to find out.

There are some people who don't even know that they might be a sociopath, they live their life normally. They won't even know something is wrong because sociopaths are that way, they don't feel guilt, remorse, or anything that may make them sorry for the things that they seem to be doing naturally.

In 1941, a book entitled "The Mask of Sanity" was written by Dr. Hervey Cleckey. Cleckey is the first one to have even written about the concept of sociopathy. Over the last few years, sociopathy and psychopathy's clinical diagnostic were studied and changed. The line between psychopath and sociopath is incredibly thin that the Diagnostic and Statistical Manual of Mental Disorders, Fourth Edition has recently renamed both condition as "Antisocial Personality Disorder".

Mental disorders normally have guidelines before they are diagnosed. Some of sociopathy's guidelines state that an individual has to be at least 18 years of age to be diagnosed, and the patient has to have had several episodes and proof that they are indeed a sociopath that was apparent even before they were 15 years old.

Specifically, Antisocial Personality Disorder has 7 key guidelines to diagnosing it, but it is for the Doctors' use and for them to determine if the patient really has this disorder or not.

Going back to the book, Cleckey wrote 16 questions that you can ask yourself to determine if you are a sociopath, you don't have to be a doctor, just answer the questions below.

Do you think you are charming and intelligent, superficially?

Superficial charm and intelligence is the over-rated belief of one person in himself. People who are superficially charming are those who are smooth, slick and verbally facile. This means that they are never shy, they believe in themselves too much.

Some questions to ask yourself are: Are you never shy? Do you always find it easy to say anything you want without ever being self-conscious or afraid? One other question to ask yourself is if you never get tongue-tied or something like that whenever you speak.

Sociopaths have let themselves free from all the normal talking norms that is normally followed. Therefore they remain to appear charming and intelligent while they talk because they seem to always have themselves together. Or on some other instances, they remain to see themselves as superficially charming and intelligent when it comes to speaking with people.

Do you sometimes have any kind of irrational thinking or delusions?

Irrational thoughts are what our brains do when it is on auto-pilot, it does not necessarily have to be well thought of, but because of something that happened, and our brains come up with a result that may paralyze us with fear.

If you are a sociopath you will not find any of these things familiar, sociopaths are immune to irrational thought because they are indeed always rational. Even to the point of hurting other people, they remain rational up to the end.

The reason behind this is that they usually don't carry any guilt or remorse with them. So if they have to do something, it always has to be the rational choice, no matter who they will hurt or no matter what will happen to other people if they do it. They always stick to the rational.

Do you have neuroses or are you overly nervous?

Neuroses is a kind of psychological state wherein you are filled with excessive insecurity and anxiety. This feelings usually comes with a number of defense mechanisms that make you look defensive even when you are not in danger of getting hurt or something. Being overly anxious is the same, you are filled with fears that may paralyze you and stop you from doing your everyday work because of fear.

If you are a sociopath, you shouldn't have ever experienced any of the above mentioned traits. Sociopaths are generally risk-takers, they are not afraid and they are never afraid to take risks.

In the mind of a sociopath, no matter what happens if he does this, he will be able to accept it and deal with it, after all he is superior and he never experiences any fear or any other feelings.

Do you think you are reliable?

Being reliable is closely knit to being responsible. If you are responsible and if you repeatedly honor and live up to something you said you will do, you will start to appear reliable to people. People will start to believe you and rely more things and feelings on you.

Sociopaths are unable to be reliable. They are unreliable to the extent that nobody believes them anymore. They tend to say something and commit to a lot of things that they actually don't end up doing. Even if they fail to do it, it won't matter to them as they will not feel any remorse that they let people down.

In a sociopath's mind, rely on me or not, I will be able to continue living my life. If you don't deal with the fact that I let you down somehow, I won't care.

Do you find it easy to say insincere things or tell lies?

Lying has various levels, there are these socially acceptable white lies that are done by almost everybody to avoid a greater problem. These lies are done in desperate measures only. These are done only to avoid greater misunderstandings or to avoid hurting anybody.

Sociopaths, on the other hand are more prone to lying, they don't need a concrete reason to do so, and they just do it as naturally as if they are telling a story.

Sociopaths' lying can be moderate or extreme. Moderate lying are those that are crafty, clever, shrewd, sly or cunning. Whereas extreme lying are often deceptive, underhanded, deceitful, manipulative, unscrupulous and dishonest.

In their minds, these lies are normal, they think that they are somewhat better than other people because they can lie and get what they want by doing so.

Do you feel shame or remorse?

Guilt is the feeling a person gets when they know that they are responsible for something or when they know they are at fault. When there is someone in the picture and that someone got hurt, a person who feels guilty will naturally feel remorse for the person who got hurt. That is the feeling of being sorry about what happened to the person.

Sociopath never feels guilty or remorse. Even if they are caught red-handed doing something, they won't care. Doing something that resulted to someone getting hurt or getting so affected, are also not something to feel guilty about for sociopaths.

The way they see it, they are eligible for what they are experiencing now, they deserve the position they have now and everything that they have now. It doesn't matter who has to get hurt while they were trying to reach it.

Do you behave as an anti-social without any good reasons at all?

Do you hate hanging out with people? When everyone your age spends all their time socializing and meeting new friends, do you find yourself at home, alone and not wanting to talk to anybody? Do you hate it when you have to socialize like in family gatherings or parties?

Sociopaths are anti-social. They don't want to be around with people, when you ask them why, they won't be able to give you a straight answer, because they don't know why either. They also have poor controls over their emotions. They get irritable easily, maybe that is one reason why they don't want to hang out with people, because they get mad easily with everybody.

They think that they are above anybody else and they do not need to interact with the crowd. They will be ok on their own.

Do you feel like you fail to learn from experience and that your judgement is poor?

When people get reprimanded for something wrong that they do, their normal reaction is to learn from it and never do it again, especially when they got severely punished for doing it.

Sociopaths often think that they are smarter than that of everyone else. They think that no matter what they do, they won't get caught. Or even if they do get caught, they will not feel that it is a punishment for them. After the punishment, they will just think that everything's back to normal.

In their mind, since I got out after your punishment, why should I learn? I will still do it again, next time I won't let you catch me. That is why they are viewed as people who don't learn from experience, when in fact they just don't care.

Do you think you are not capable of love and that you are egocentric?

Egocentric is regarding or having yourself the center of everything in existence. A person who is egocentric usually disregards every social norm, every belief and interests of other people. All that is important to him is himself and what he wants.

Sociopaths are egocentric. They only think about themselves. They don't care about what other people may think of them and they don't care if they are stepping on other people's tradition, faith, or even attitude and interest. Aside from being egocentric, sociopaths are incapable of falling in love.

They can't really love anybody else since they have no regard for anybody except themselves. They feel that nobody deserves their love but themselves. Nobody is above them, so therefore, no one can be given the love that they can give.

Do you think you lack the capability to react emotionally?

When something emotionally moving happens, people can't help but become emotional. Sometimes, just watching somebody else cry make tears roll down our cheeks even without us noticing it. When you know someone who is going through some tough time, it is you instinct to feel sympathetic over him and try to console him.

Sociopaths are not capable of that. They lack the capability of reacting emotionally. They can look at someone who had just lost a loved one with such cold eye that they will appear mean. Sometimes, they do feel sad, but they do not show these emotions the way we are used to seeing other people's emotions.

When asked about it, they don't even know they are like that. They just didn't feel emotional, or they just could not react emotionally like how other people would normally react.

Do you feel like you lack insight?

Insight is the ability to comprehend something that happens depending on the cause that made it like that. Sometimes, there are just some things that we can't control. Everything that happens has its own "cause-effect" reason why it happened and no matter how much we don't like it, we just have to accept it.

Sociopaths are not able to do so. They are unable to comprehend that things happen for a reason. If something happens that is a bit different from what they are expecting to happen, it is easy for them to lose their cool and get mad at anyone even if it is not anyone's fault in reality.

Since they don't have the capability to owe up even if they have a mistake, when something happens they tend to blame it on whoever they can, just so they have something to blame.

Do you think that you are overly responsive when it comes to other people?

During the course of the day, we naturally go through a series of encounters with other people. It might be while we are at work, while we are on the way to work or even while we are still at home. These encounters requires social communication that may or may not prolong the conversation or result to them paying attention to you.

Sociopaths do not like that. In the course of their day, they tend to fake their reactions to people. They tend to react the way that they think other people expects them to. They do not want to be paid attention to.

They would even go to the point of having no social contact for a day and just fake reactions for people just so they won't be "seen".

Do you feel that you are a party fiend and a meaningless sex machine?

Crazy party fiends are those that exhibit such behavior that is not socially inviting behavior when out in a party. This may happen with or without alcohol. These behaviors are fantastic but are uninviting for other people to interact with you.

Sociopaths are like that, they are anti-social, but when it comes to the point that they actually go to parties, they certainly have something up in their sleeves. They tend to become a crazy party fiend and engage in their uninviting behavior no matter if they had too much to drink or not.

During these parties, sociopaths also crave for sex, even meaningless one, more than the other people his or her age. They tend to engage with people and use their manipulative lying skills just to have them in bed. Sometimes they can't help it, they just want to have sex.

Do you fake suicide threats just to get what you want?

Suicide tendencies are prevalent in people who are diagnosed with mental illness, people with bipolar most often than not have suicide tendencies whenever they feel depressed, they tend to look at things as if they have no chance in getting a better life anymore, and the only way to escape the hell they are in is to end their life. They do not want anybody to know, they just do it when they feel the need to.

Sociopaths on the other hand broadcasts their suicide threats. No, they do not have suicidal tendencies, but they do have a cunning mind that they know these threats can get them what they want.

They feel that they are above other people. They find it hard to believe when people don't give them what they want, or when things don't go their way. So their tendency is to not give up and accept, but to manipulate the situation by faking a suicide attempt, just so some of the circumstances around them will change, and people will think that they have no choice but to give them what they want.

Do you think your sex life is not personal?

Sex is an act that two people who are in love do. Over the course of a person's life, they can have numerous sexual partners. This may be because they have jumped from lover to lover. They may have loved several people, though not at the same time, but this is possible. It is possible for a person to have sex with several people, but these sex acts are all personal and in such levels as that of people making love.

Sociopaths on the other hand engage in sex too, but that's it. They just engage in sex without any personal connection or any love involved. They are capable of doing that. They can jump from sexual relationship to another without being attached or in love.

For them, they just have to have sex. Most of the time, they tend to use their manipulative skills just to have sex with somebody. Their sex life is often trivial, poorly integrated or just plain impersonal.

Do you feel like you don't have a life plan?

A life plan is something that keeps people going for the rest of their life. They feel that they are on the right path. A long term engagement and commitment to follow the plan is a good way for them to gauge whether they are doing good in life or not.

This is what sociopaths fail to have. They don't have a life plan, or if they do they always fail to follow it. They would eventually fall off the wagon after following it for a short period of time, they tend to get bored about something when it is becoming a routine.

Sociopaths are also incapable of nurturing a long term relationship. Anything that requires a long term commitment is something that sociopaths cannot seem to handle.

This may be in terms of their jobs, their relationships, and even their marriage. They fail in having these long term commitments because they get bored easily.

These are the 16 questions that are found in Cleckey's book. These are used to diagnose whether a patient is a sociopath or not. There is no 100% surefire way to diagnosing if you have sociopathy by yourself, in fact, you may even lie your way through these series of questions.

But if you honestly think that you recognized a number, or all of these questions, then it might be best to ask for professional help. This is not meant to make you feel bad about yourself, these are meant for you to determine whether you are going to seek for help now.

These questions are used but it is not fail-proof, the fact that sociopaths know that of they pass this test, they will either be taken to a mental institution or a prison is enough fact to make them lie their way through. They can even fake some parts of their life just so people around them will think that they are ok and they are doing well with their lives.

Sociopaths have the skills to be successful in life. They often use it to be successful and avoid any encounter with the professionals and risks of going to prison or any mental institute that people might think they belong to.

Chapter 21: Borderline Personality Disorder – The Symptoms, Treatment Methods And Future Prospects

This disorder also falls into the category B range of personality disorders. It is also known as Emotionally Unstable Personality Disorder. This type of personality disorder is recognisable by the speed of mood changes and the general inability to build relationships. This is compounded as sufferers tend to have very unstable behavioural patterns.

The majority of sufferers will display the following symptoms:

Intense and Rapid emotional responses

Someone who has a borderline personality is likely to experience a rapid shift in emotion. This is because they are deeply affected by emotional influences and their feelings stay with them for a long time. The smallest of acts can trigger an emotional response which may seem completely over the top for the situation.

In fact, their emotional response is so intense that they will often appear to be at one end of the scale or another; either exceptionally enthusiastic, loving and idealistic or extremely anxious, angry, depressed or even feeling guilty. In effect, where the average person would experience a mild embarrassment; they feel an acute sense of shame or humiliation.

These strong emotional responses can lead sufferers to be very sensitive regarding any incident of failure, rejection or even feeling isolated; they will also struggle to cope with these negative emotions and may become a suicide risk or consider ways of harming themselves.

The condition can be made worse as sufferers become aware of how drastic and damaging their negative reactions are; this will often lead them to shut down their negative responses rather than be unable to deal with them. Unfortunately, negative responses are an important and healthy part of the human make-up; ignoring them is the same as ignoring the issue and will leave them unable to notice or address any issue.

The extreme emotions usually felt by people with this disorder will often lead to feeling a lack of identity, victimisation and even self destruction. This can be demonstrated through their impulse behaviour with little or no regard of the risk involved.

Impulsive Behaviour which can often be harmful

The range of impulsive behaviour displayed by those suffering from this disorder is broad; it can include quitting a good job, simply leaving their house, neighbourhood or city and running away or indulging in reckless driving and spending. In fact, their impulsive behaviour will usually have a sexual connotation and is likely to include unprotected sex with multiple partners; any opportunity will be taken, regardless as to whether it is worthwhile or not.

This impulsive behaviour can also lead to a dependency on alcohol, drugs or the development of an eating disorder.

The impulsive behaviour is usually a reaction to the intense emotional feelings they experience; it is their attempt to deal with these emotions by blocking them out and focusing on something different. The impulsive behaviour is often followed by a period of shame and guilt at their actions. Unfortunately, this emotional response will create a desire to engage in more impulsive behaviour to rid them of the emotional pain. It becomes a never ending circle, with the emotions becoming stronger each time they experience them. It can, ultimately be the trigger for more destructive behaviour such as self harm or even suicide.

A Lack of Self-Worth

The inability for someone with this disorder to stop this cycle will be damaging to their own self image and sense of self-worth. They will feel inferior and incapable of controlling their own life and destiny. In fact, this can frequently lead to a further cycle of the impulsive behaviour as they attempt to shut out the emotional pain of their inability to control their own life.

Unfortunately, this disorder can lead to a depressing, never ending cycle of guilt, shame and impulsive behaviour. Many sufferers start self harming in order to punish themselves for their behaviour. It can also be to ensure they are still capable of experiencing normal feelings such as pain, or, it can be to distract them from the emotional pain and complications of their circumstances.

Suicide is sometimes seen as the best option and is contemplated when the sufferer believes they will be better off dead.

These thoughts and feelings are made worse by the fact that most people with this disorder have a lack of self-worth. This stems from a difficulty establishing and knowing what goals they have in the short and long term and, even knowing what their own values and beliefs are.

Relationship Issues

Someone who is suffering from borderline personality disorder is likely to switch quickly from like to hate when dealing with relationships. This is partly because much of what they do is seen in a black and white context; there is no middle ground. They will quickly latch onto someone who expresses gratitude or appreciation of their work or hobbies. However, if this person or someone else attempts to criticise them or appears hurtful, they will instantly turn to anger and even hate.

This switch in personality, combined with the constantly shifting mood patterns they experience, will make it very difficult for a sufferer to connect, build and maintain relationships with colleagues, friends and even family.

Aggressive Behaviour

The constantly shifting moods and awareness of people's criticisms will often leave sufferers of this disorder believing that the world is a dangerous and bad place. This leads to elevated stress levels and sufferers often link this to their relationships creating conflict. As the conflict escalates the relationship can collapse and sufferers can become extremely aggressive. This, of course, places more strain on their relationship and starts a self-fulfilling cycle where the relationship is doomed to fail.

Abandonment Issues

A common side effect of low self esteem is the need to cling to others and obtain reassurance from this. This can be assurance of their own self worth or that the person will always be there for them; no matter what. Should any occurrence happens which, in their mind, could lead to them being left alone they will react very strongly. They have a deep seated fear of being abandoned and this will quickly trigger an aggressive and negative response; which can trigger a negative downward cycle.

A real or perceived abandonment can also cause someone with this disorder to self harm as a way of obtaining attention and preventing the person from leaving them.

Treating the Condition

Although there has been a huge amount of research into the causes of this personality disorder; there has been no conclusive evidence to suggest that it is caused by a specific item. Upbringing and genes are considered to partly responsible and there is an increased risk of developing this condition if you are directly related to someone who has it.

Once diagnosed, via a qualified medical professional, the usual treatment method is through a mixture of psychotherapy and medication.

The first step is almost always several meetings with a counsellor, this is to build trust and establish a rapport. Ideally this will help the sufferer to open up concerning their emotions and feelings of guilt and shame. The counsellor can then decide on the best route forward:

Dialectical Behavioural Therapy

This type of therapy will introduce a wide range of skills which can be practiced by the sufferer. The intention, by mastering these skills, is to control the intense emotional responses. Controlling these will allow the sufferer to reduce their need to harm themselves or to feel guilty or ashamed. The therapy teaches sufferers how to control their responses; it allows them to create a balance between which behaviours are acceptable and which need to be changed.

This has been shown to be the most effective method of treating Borderline personality disorder and involves both individual and group therapy sessions.

Cognitive Behavioural Therapy

This therapy will help a sufferer to change the way they think and behave. It will focus on the negative aspects which someone with this disorder has about themselves; an even about others. It will help them to change the way they see themselves, others and the situations they find themselves in. This, in turn, will allow them to find alternative ways of dealing with an issue; this has been shown to be of great assistance in reducing incidents of self harm and mood swings.

Mentalization Based Therapy

This therapy provides another opportunity for a sufferer to talk about their experiences and look at possible solutions. In particular this therapy will focus on understanding the thoughts and feelings of others. Learning to appreciate how others perceive the various encounters provides a useful guide for dealing with these situations in a more sympathetic manner which will naturally create a better solution.

Transference Focused Therapy

In these sessions the therapist will concentrate on creating scenarios and encounters between them and the sufferer. From these encounters they will work out a solution together. These examples can then be used and applied to the everyday conversations and situations that the sufferer finds themselves in.

Medications

These are not usually prescribed until the behavioural therapies have started to have an effect on the sufferer. There is no medication which can heal someone from a personality disorder. However, there are medications designed to treat depression, anxiety and even impulse behaviour. The purpose of treating these symptoms is to keep a sufferer focused on the key issues without being distracted by their emotional responses.

Most medications have side effects and it is a good idea to talk through these through with the doctor first to ensure they will not make the symptoms worse.

Studies have also suggested that the use of Omega 3 Fatty acids can help to alleviate the symptoms of borderline personality disorder. But there is not yet any confirmation of this fact.

Self-Help

As with any medical condition or personality disorder, one of the most effective treatment methods is to look after yourself. Avoiding other illnesses and being in the best condition possible will increase your chances of learning to control your personality disorder and adapting to living a fulfilling, high quality lifestyle.

If a sufferer has experienced extreme symptoms connected with this disorder or is at risk of self-harming, it is possible for a doctor to hospitalise the sufferer. This is not common practice as it is not believed to be beneficial in most cases. However, at times this can be the right option to allow treatment to start.

It is important to note that the treatment for this disorder can be completed in months or may take years; it is dependent upon how the sufferer responds and whether they want to recover. No matter how long or short the treatment is, someone who suffers from this disorder will need to monitor themselves for the rest of their life.

Conclusion

Thanks again for downloading this book!

First of all, I hope the information presented here has given you a new, clear perspective about sociopathy. As researchers note, four percent of the general population are sociopaths. In other words, the chance of encountering one is not impossible.

In dealing with a sociopath, understanding his or her nature is the first step. And, may the things shared in this book become helpful to you along the way. Armed with the right information, you can better protect yourself if it becomes necessary.

Second, sociopathy is a heavy cross to bear. It stays with a person for the rest of his lifetime. While full-blown sociopathy may be quite impossible to correct, stopping the development of sociopathy is perfectly possible at its early onset. Awareness of the warning signs can help you prevent a loved one from turning out differently than the rest.

Finally, please bear in mind that not all sociopaths are created the same. Their lack of guilt, shame, and remorse, as well as their self centeredness and lack of empathy for others may be their common denominators. But, not all of them have criminal tendencies.

Sociopaths may be different. But, some of them manage to do better than what is expected of them.

Thank you, and good luck!

9 781774 851272